CW00739116

Sri Lanka Style

TROPICAL DESIGN AND ARCHITECTURE

Channa Daswatte
photographs by Dominic Sansoni

PERIPLUS

Published by Periplus Editions (HK) Ltd.,
with editorial offices at 130 Joo Seng Road
#06-01, Singapore 368357.

Text © 2006 Channa Daswatte
Photos © 2006 Dominic Sansoni

All rights reserved. No part of this publi-
cation may be reproduced, stored in a
retrieval system or transmitted in any form
or by any means, electronic, mechanical,
photocopying, recording or otherwise
without prior permission of the publisher.

ISBN 13 978 0 7946 0060 0
ISBN 10 0 7946 0060 3
Printed in Singapore

Design: Mind Design

Distributed by:
Asia Pacific
Berkeley Books Pte Ltd, 130 Joo Seng
Road #06-01, Singapore 368357.
Tel: (65) 6280 3320; Fax: (65) 6280 6290
E-mail: inquiries@periplus.com.sg
www.periplus.com

North America
Tuttle Publishing, 364 Innovation Drive,
North Clarendon, Vermont 05759, USA.
Tel: (802) 773 8930; Fax: (802) 773 6993
E-mail: info@tuttlepublishing.com
www.tuttlepublishing.com

Japan
Tuttle Publishing, Yaekari Building, 3F,
5-4-12 Osaki, Shinagawa-ku, Tokyo
141-0032. Tel: (81)3 5437 0171;
Fax: (81)3 5437 0755
E-mail: tuttle-sales@gol.com

10 09 08 07
6 5 4 3

FRONT ENDPAPER
A man bears a tray of jasmine as an offering to the tooth relic in this eighteenth-
century painting in the entrance corridor
of the Temple of the Tooth in Kandy.

BACK ENDPAPER
A Sinhalese woman dressed in Portuguese
style appears at a window in a nineteenth-
century painting at the Kataluwa Temple
near Galle.

PAGE 1
A nineteenth-century office chair and jackwood sideboard in the Club Villa, Bentota
(page 190).

PAGE 2
The bazaar-like sitting area in the Cinnamon
House, Galle Fort (page 92).

PAGES 4–5
The grand staircase leading up to the Galle
Face Court Dome, Colombo (page 74).

Contents

The Serendipitous Isle

As the haze of twilight descends on Kandy ("mountain"), the citadel of the last kings of Sri Lanka, called by many Sinhalese people Mahanuwara or the "great city," the oboes and rolling drums that mark the evening worship at the sacred Temple of the Tooth Relic reverberate throughout the valley. On the northern slope of this valley, in a place of worship planned and built by missionary teachers of an Anglican Christian school, the sound of evensong melds with that of the temple drums. This is a typical example of the fusion that is contemporary Sri Lankan style. The chapel for Trinity College is built of warm honey-colored granite that was brought in from a quarry 5 miles (8 km) away by elephants, and designed by the British Vice-Principal Gaster. Started in 1922, it simply copies and uses for a different purpose the most common of vernacular Sri Lankan buildings—the open pavilion.

The pavilion is the quintessential Sri Lankan building. From the simple wayside shelter (*ambalama*) that dots the pilgrim routes, to the drumming halls of the pilgrimage centers, right up to the very center of government, the Magul Maduwa (Hall of Royal Audience), open-sided pavilions with huge overhanging roofs were the central spaces for life in Sri Lanka. The salubrious climate only required that a dwelling function as an umbrella, protecting its occupants from the sun and rain, while allowing air to enter.

These spaces contained nothing more or less than the objects that were essential for everyday life. Each object, however, was beautifully crafted to suit its purpose and the means of the occupant. A palpable sense of peace and discipline pervaded the atmosphere. This was a result of a complete control and discipline of making space and putting

material together. The only bounded enclosed space in many of these traditional dwellings was perhaps to store things. Even today, most Sri Lankan village houses have no more than one enclosed space.

The village houses and dwellings of the populous were of the simplest possible construction and design: wattle-and-daub (*warichchi*) structures carefully covered over with mud and cow dung and roofed with plaited coconut fronds. Traditionally, only the building of the feudal élite and religious structures had lime-washed walls and clay shingle roofs. Thus, while these buildings stood out against the lush green landscape, along with the brilliant saffron robes of the monks, those of the majority of the people blended back into the landscape. Essentially a non-urban architecture, these vernacular structures were placed with great skill in relation to each other on the landscape. This is epitomized by the thirteenth-century temple and monastery of Lankatillake outside Kandy.

Whilst residential interiors of traditional houses were plain and contained only the beautifully crafted utensils and objects of everyday life, the interiors of religious and ritual buildings were in complete contrast. Dealing with the supra mundane, these interiors are a fantasy of color and pattern: here, polychrome walls and statues compete with brilliantly colored temple hanging cloths and curtains.

The accommodation of ritual functions in other buildings was accompanied by temporary decorations such as the Rali Palamas, literally "bridges of waves," made from bright-colored calico, usually the traditional colors of red and white, and bamboo frames. Other temporary decorative structures accompany various ritual functions such as funerals,

RIGHT
Intricately carved and painted *pekada* column capitals and ceiling support the even more highly embellished roof structure at the Temple of the Tooth in Kandy.

weddings and curative practices like the Sanni Yakkumas and Bali ceremonies that are performed to avert disease and other disasters. These are amplified by the brilliant colors of the costumes. The temporary decorations that accompany Christian religious feasts, such as arches of coconuts and flowers, sometimes remind one of northern Spain or Portugal, from whence Catholicism was introduced to the island in the sixteenth century. Others are adaptations of Eastern practices such as the decoration of a mast that represents a tree of flags, which derives from the Eastern practice of decorating sacred trees. Strings of mango leaves over a door with a pair of banana trees in fruit mark Hindu households on the religious holidays of those believers.

The colonial tradition, like in most other Asian situations, adopted local building methods and techniques. These resulted in sensible buildings that addressed the issue of living in a tropical environment. The colonials also introduced principles of classical order to the construction of houses. Both in planning and detail, classical principles began to be absorbed by Sri Lankan builders. By the end of the eighteenth century, Sri Lankan architecture was a unique blend of local construction tradition and Western classical planning principles. This pervaded the whole gamut of architecture, from the smallest wayside shop to the most extravagant mansions of the local ruling class, the Ratemahatayas and Mudliyars.

Although the monsoon climate of the Indian subcontinent seemed both beneficial and beautiful, the heat and humidity, aided by termites and fungus, destroyed even the most solid of materials. This spurred craftsmen to employ easily renewable material on decorations. One of the simplest materials available for finishing a house on this coral reef-rimmed island was lime wash or *hunu*. Occasional color came from the use of a mud-based *samara* or yellow ochre paint. Doors were painted with a variety of vegetable dyes stabilized with *dummala* resin.

RIGHT
The cool interior of the former horse stalls at the old manor house of Horagalla (page 42) has been converted into the main sitting room, with four main areas for sitting, two up and two down. At one end of the room, a small cement-finished staircase leads to the upper levels which are connected by a bridge-like part of the original hayloft.

The British colonial period saw a continuation of this tradition at one level, where the fusion of Portuguese and Dutch conventions were allowed to continue in everyday buildings. However, in buildings of state, current British tastes were imposed, as elsewhere in the Empire. The fall-out from this was the introduction of a further layer of eclecticism in Sri Lankan style and architecture. Invoking a clause in the Kandyan Convention of 1815, in which the last independent Sri Lankan kingdom was ceded to the British, the British monarch was made protector of the faith of Buddhism and portraits of Queen Victoria appeared over the central entrances to Buddhist shrine rooms. Gothic cathedrals housed vast polychrome statues of the Buddha, whilst Victorian Italianate façades adorned mosques.

During the twentieth century, more and more outside influences flooded in and the Sri Lankan style continued to absorb and evolve. Numerous individuals influenced this development. Comte de Mauny, the European aristocrat who settled in Sri Lanka in the 1920s on an island off the southern coast, designed his own eccentric but truly local house. Through his designs for furniture and gardens for other people, the local élite adopted his style and sensibility.

Around the same time, Bevis Bawa, one of the ADCs to the then governor of Ceylon, inherited a property from his father and decided to live a life of leisure in the country and create for himself the elegant house and garden of Brief. Here, he let loose his fantasies and incredible talents as an amateur architect, interior designer and gardener, abandoning form and interior design principles in a lascivious embrace of landscape, sunshine and rain. The old introverted plantation bungalow was completely opened out and wrapped around in pergolas and verandas to create space that is no longer inside or outside. Around this, he laid out his own fantasy of a tropical garden: hidden belvederes in lush tropical vegetation, moon gates and courtyards paved with cement stones on which leaf impressions were frozen in time. The lifestyle of Bevis Bawa attracted a large number of eclectic travelers to his house where he entertained them and regaled them with his incredible wit and tales.

Amongst them was Donald Friend, the precociously talented Australian artist and writer, who came for the weekend in 1957 and stayed on for several years in Bevis's garage; he was later to live in Bali for fourteen years. His artistic contributions are dotted around Bevis's garden and that of his brother Geoffrey. Bevis eventually wrote a regular piece for a local newspaper on gardening and, like the count, went on to design and plant several outstanding gardens for friends and later for larger institutions. One that survives him is that of the Sigiriya Village near the ancient archaeological site of the same name.

Lionel Wendt was a unique figure in the early realization of Sri Lankan contemporary art and design. A gifted pianist, he took up photography and went on to become one of the most prolific and best-known practitioners of that art in the country. His immense energy fired the imagination of many contemporary artists, in particular George Keyt, who worked closely with Wendt on several occasions. Wendt's eye for detail in recording the beauty of his country and its people drew the attention of the public to their own style and

culture in regular portfolios of photographs in newspaper supplements. Wendt's photographs publicly celebrated all that was beautiful in what was still in the 1930s and 1940s a traditional culture.

Wendt was instrumental in bringing together the 43rd Group. This group of artists and writers met to explore the problems of introducing modern art within the context of a traditional and non-Western culture. The work of Ivan Peiris, Justin Dereniyagala and George Keyt, amongst others, began a style and school of Sri Lankan painting that celebrated the everyday.

A fringe member of this art group was Andrew Boyd, who started as a tea taster but went on to become one of the first modern architects of Ceylon before returning to Britain after the war to work for the Greater London Council. His interest in architecture was largely inspired by Sri Lankan vernacular buildings, which he described in a series of articles in Sri Lankan newspapers. He was struck by the similarity of simple traditional buildings to the clean functionalism of the modernist style.

OPPOSITE
The entrance to the Sandella or Garden Room at Lunuganga (page 154), the legendary garden estate of Geoffrey Bawa, is flanked by two antique columns recycled from old buildings—as are the rest of the architectural elements in the building.

ABOVE
The original entrance hallway at 79, Leyn Baan Street in Galle Fort (page 98) now doubles as a formal dining room. Its walls, hung with a collection of paintings done for the owner by an Indonesian artist, are complemented by mirrors in rustic frames.

This interest in traditional architecture was further developed by Minette de Silva. Coming back to practice in Sri Lanka after her studies at the Architectural Association in London, and striking up a friendship with Le Corbusier, who called her "my little bird," she set out to discover ways of making and doing things which would be both new and vital and, at the same time, essentially Sri Lankan. These first attempts at a deliberate fusion encouraged local craftsmen to engage with contemporary buildings. Winding modernist staircases lined in lac-work balusters, ethereal carved screens separating otherwise flowing space, and lamp niches built into load-bearing walls built of earth blocks (*kabook*) evoked a unique modernist Sri Lankan style. Local handlooms designed and executed by de Silva and an English designer friend adorned her walls and doorways. This search for a modern Asian identity in design and style resulted in her collaborating, along with her sister Anil and Mulk Raj Anand, in the Modern Art Research Group in Bombay, which published one of Asia's first art magazines, *Marg*.

In 1948, a young lawyer turned world traveler returned from his wanderings to settle down to a more sedate life in his native Ceylon, which was then slowly drifting in its own inimitably gentle manner towards independence. Having bought a small rubber plantation on a promontory by a lake, Geoffrey Bawa promptly cut down the rubber trees in order to make his own version of an earthly paradise. A few years on, after some prodding from a visiting cousin, he decided to embark on a career in architecture. At the conclusion of his formal education, Bawa returned to Sri Lanka to start a career that was to reshape the ideals of Sri Lankan architectural and design thinking. In addition to his vast experience of architecture and style culled from his travels, one of his first clients, who wanted a "different" house to those being built at the time, showed him around several of her ancestral homes. This, along with memories of his own childhood homes, awakened his interest in local architectural traditions.

This interest in his roots was taken up by his young partner, Danish architect Ulrik Plesner, who early in his career, in 1957, had moved to Sri Lanka to work in the office of Minette de Silva. Plesner had grown up with the Sandinavian modernism of the early 1950s, which valued simple abstract functionalism and honest use of natural materials. With his friend Barbara Sansoni, Plesner gathered together a group of young architects who

sought out and recorded many vernacular buildings. Their work resulted—almost fifty years later—in the wonderful book *The Architecture of an Island*. Their research also fed back directly into the designs which Bawa and Plesner produced during their productive partnership in the period 1959–1965. Perhaps Bawa's most evocative works from this time were the Ena de Silva house in 1960 and the Bentota Beach Hotel of 1969. His inclusive and eclectic style was to set the trend of design and style in the 1960s and 1970s. His biographer Brian Bruce Taylor described Bawa as one of the supreme examples of an architect of our times: "Highly personal in his approach, evoking the pleasures of the senses that go hand in hand with climate, landscape and culture, Bawa brings together an appreciation of the Western humanist tradition in architecture with local needs and lifestyles."

Some of the artists and crafts people who worked with and around Geoffrey Bawa helped to create a new style of the everyday. The vibrant colors of a Barbara Sansoni fabric are still a watchword of Sri Lankan design. The contemporary batiks by Ena de Silva virtually invented a Sri Lankan tradition within this ancient art form from Southeast Asia. Laki Senanayake was someone who straddled the world of architecture, fine art and craftsmanship. Originally an architectural assistant of Geoffrey Bawa, he became a collaborator of Ena de Silva and went on to become one of Sri Lanka's most respected artists and landscape designers.

Contemporary Sri Lankan style is a fusion, as it has always been, befitting the island's status as an entrepôt of Indian ocean trade from times immemorial, the island of the legendary Tarshish from which was exported the jewels for Solomon to woo the queen of Sheba. It is an all-inclusive style that continues to change and realign itself to the various movements and patterns of world culture, but reinventing itself with a unique Sri Lankan twist.

Contemporary designers draw from as many influences and inspirations as anywhere else in the world. However, the essential ingredients that best accommodate life and style in Sri Lanka still shine through, with spaces left open to the environment, and with an emphasis on simplcity in the disposition of space and in décor. Similarly, the stock in contemporary design emporia at first glance appears the same as that in other stores worldwide. However, a closer examination reveals a serendipitous combination of elements that is uniquely of the island.

Vernacular and Colonial Inspirations

innamon. The very sound of the word conjures up images of tropical allure. In the sixteenth century, the trade in the queen of Eastern spices, *Cinnamonium Zeylanicum*, was the sole prerogative of the kings of Ceylon and Arab traders, but with the rise of the Ottoman Empire and its control over land routes to the East and the subsequent discovery of sea routes, Western traders began to deal directly with the East—with marked repercussions on the history and culture of Sri Lanka, many apparent to this day.

November 1505 was a critical moment in the history of the country. The life of the inhabitants, indeed the very composition of its people, would change dramatically. Swept by monsoon winds, three Portuguese caravels under the command of Lorenzo de Almeida found landfall near the port of Colombo. Their now-legendary journey to meet the King of Ceylon, Bhuwenaka Bahu IV, at Kotte, the then and present capital of Ceylon, would begin 500 years of links with the colonial powers of Europe. Having won concessions from Bhuwenaka Bahu to establish a small warehouse in the solely Arab port of Colombo, the Portuguese went on to build a fort and, eventually, to take control of the maritime areas of Sri Lanka.

Old prints and illustrations of the Portuguese city of Colombo show a Mediterranean city of churches and closely built urban streets within the fortified area. The houses reveal classic northern Iberian features, with heavy bases and timbered upper parts. Although very few physical artifacts remain from this era, either in Colombo or in other areas under Portuguese suzerainty, the Portuguese legacy is apparent in the baroque churches of the Catholic faith and in the religious icons within them. What endures is the Portuguese tradition of building and its distinctly Indo-Portuguese style of furniture, which were to profoundly influence succeeding colonial cultures, and its language and food, which are today very much a part of Sri Lankan culture.

By 1658 the Dutch, who had intrigued the kings of Ceylon, now retreated to the mountain stronghold of Kandy, where they developed their own lifestyle and culture, and managed to drive the Portuguese out of Sri Lanka. Much to the regret of Kirthi Sri Rajasinghe, the King of Kandy, the Dutch decided to remain in the country and develop and eventually monopolize the spice trade. As with the Portuguese, Dutch styles of building, their food and language have become an integral part of Sri Lankan vernacular culture, and large numbers of distinctly Dutch-period

buildings and furniture survive to this day. However, Dutch colonial style in Sri Lanka, while retaining some influences from the Netherlands, is a distinctly recognizable fusion, influenced by developments in their two most important Dutch overseas possessions, Batavia and the Cape in South Africa. Batavian influences include the use of tiles and stucco and the sweeping high-pitched roofs, while some architectural elements and much of the furniture share features with that of the Cape. Early Dutch-period doors, for instance, are austere and bear resemblance to the joinery of the farmhouses of the Cape, whereas later examples are finer with smaller panes of shuttered glass.

What mostly remains from the Dutch colonial period are residential buildings, many of them town houses built within the fortress towns, others suburban villas. The town houses usually comprise four main living spaces

running from the street to a back courtyard garden, joined by a service wing, a series of spaces along one side of the courtyard. The front veranda or *istppuwa*—the *stoep* of the Dutch—that opened directly on to the road, usually leads through a narrow high hall, flanked by two rooms, into a great *zaal* or hall, which in turn opens to a veranda facing the inner garden. The main living rooms are always generously proportioned, with high roofs sealed off with timber planks. The sub-urban villas have a similar, though less rigid, arrangement of spaces than their urban counterparts. The formal geometric plans of these houses may have been influenced by the Palladian fashions sweeping northern Europe, but may equally have been influenced by traditional Sinhalese manor houses and palaces.

Dutch-period architecture was very much distinguished by its use of simple, vernacular materials. Thick walls were made of stone or laterite laid in a mud or mud-and-lime mortar and then heavily plastered with coral lime, which was then either lime-washed or washed with *samara*, the distinctly ochre color prevalent in many old buildings. Sweeping timber-framed roofs supported by round columns were finished with a covering of half-round *sinhala* terracotta tiles laid on thin timber slats—now synonymous with Sri Lankan architecture but possibly first introduced by the Arabs and later adopted by both the Portuguese and Dutch. Doors and windows were made from heavy sectioned jackwood joinery. Although the details have changed over time, these elements are clearly visible in the architecture in other Dutch colonies of the period and in parallel architectural developments in Europe. The few civic buildings that do survive from the period have a distinctly utilitarian appearance, a plain no-nonsense architecture to serve the puritan

PREVIOUS PAGE
Pargetting or plasterwork in low relief is common in most nineteenth-century religious buildings on the coastal plain. Here, the façade of a Buddhist temple bears myriad encrustations, including a coat of arms derived from the colonial British but with lions on both sides and a stupa surmounting the shield.

BELOW
This painting, in the style of the southern school, clearly shows traditional seventeenth-century dress. Sarongs from Burma and *somana* cloth from the East India trade are worn as lungi, along with Western-inspired jackets. The tortoiseshell hair combs indicate the high status of these men.

17

Calvinist culture and work ethic. In the churches that survived, however, the distinct baroque style then prevalent in European ecclesiastical architecture is manifested.

Dutch-period furniture is particularly noteworthy. The spindly Indo-Portuguese style gives way to a much heavier and exuberant baroque, which has come to be considered distinctly Sri Lankan, although some styles of furniture are found in the Cape colony and Batavia. The style, however, falls short of becoming rococo. even though a Dutch shell motif finds its way into most of the furniture of the period. Huge four-poster beds spread and hung with pure white linen lined with Flemish lace are a notable feature of the interiors of the period. The art of making this lace, known as *beeralu*, survives in many of the coastal areas of Sri Lanka.

At the end of the eighteenth century, the British displaced the Dutch as the colonial masters of Sri Lanka. Initially, the existing Portuguese and Dutch building traditions persisted, largely because the building industry was controlled by Portuguese Burghers, but as the nineteenth century progressed the British began to impose the styles of their empire. While neighboring India indulged in the full flight of Victorian fancy, the British in Ceylon preferred to use neoclassical styles in their public buildings, and include adaptations to local climatic conditions. Unlike the

Dutch who were happy simply to trade for spices, the British set about creating a plantation economy on a massive scale. British colonial style is best exemplified in the still-extant plantation bungalows and planters' clubs in the hill stations of Sri Lanka where the British administrators attempted to re-create a life as close as possible to that of home. Bungalows set in immaculate lawns trimmed with petunias, foxgloves and other temperate plants are still a part of the scene in the hills.

The early bungalows were very plain affairs: simple two-roomed structures with a veranda. The arrival of British wives changed all this. The British traditions of the country house were emulated in the plantation bungalows, especially the formal dining room, drawing room and suites of rooms for guests. By the early twentieth century, the British bungalow was a well-developed establishment built on two principles. One was the paramount importance of verandas all round the house as the space in which to relax and also to meet local or native acquaintances, who were never invited into the house proper. The other was the location of staff quarters at a distance from the main house, connected to it by a corridor, but placed on the leeward side of the winds so that spice-laden cooking smells would not carry to the main house. These ideals were followed in every British-period bungalow whatever its external stylization.

ABOVE
The main dining space of the Dutch House in Galle (page 32) is the back veranda. Overlooking a courtyard planted with soursop trees, the veranda is sparsely furnished with reproduction seventeenth-century Wolfendhal chairs and modern steel tables. The kitchen is located at the end.

Starchy clubs, such as the Hill Club in Nuwara Eliya, also epitomize British colonial style. Built in a sub-Lutyens "country lifestyle," the Nuwara Eliya continues to maintain a men's bar, to insist on ties and jackets at dinner, and to place hot water bottles between the bedcovers. The sweeping fairways of the Nuwara Eliya Golf Club and its wicker furniture, crisp starched linen, afternoon teas and dinners of roast beef with over-boiled vegetables are ubiquitous reminders of the British period.

During this time, furniture became less heavy and more decorative, although the new bureaucracy also demanded huge quantities of plain and functional furniture. Highly decorated transoms above doors and windows replaced the plainer designs of the Dutch. After his visit to Ceylon in the 1890s, the feathers of the Prince of Wales began to feature in many designs. Even temple architecture changed to exuberant displays of encrusted vegetation pargetted on to every possible surface. Queen Victoria herself gained the status of a minor deity, presiding amidst the foliage as part of the exuberant *makara thorana* that form the ceremonial archway over entrances into Buddhist shrines.

The later British period, however, saw a return to simplicity, particularly in bungalow construction, while the influences of the Arts and Crafts movement in Europe and also the Art Deco movement began to be felt in Sri

Lanka. For government buildings, however, the neoclassical style was favored as being most suited to the vision of a rational empire. The Kandy High Court (1860) and the Colombo Museum (1877), both built by the chief Public Works Department architect Smither, epitomize this attitude. The PWD also built a valuable stock of standard design buildings for the Ceylon government railway, which still gives the railway a unique identity. As late as 1930, the buildings for the State Assembly, later the Parliament and now the Presidential Secretariat, also designed by the PWD, used an Ionic order to embellish the grandeur of the structure.

Although architects like Edwards, Reid and Begg used the Classical style for their town hall design in 1925, by the early twentieth century they happily used Art Deco for office buildings such as the Princes Building in the Fort, and for apartment buildings such as the Galle Face Court, and employed Arts and Crafts styling for estate bungalows such as Adhisham, and even a neo-Sri Lankan style for the extensions to the Temple of the Tooth in Kandy and that of Kelaniya.

Parallel to the development of urban architecture, Sri Lankan vernacular styles also derived from the various building practices of several historic periods. The oldest and most resilient is the rural village dwelling. Other styles have been permutations and

ABOVE LEFT
The attic bedroom in the Artist's Residence in Galle (page 48) is furnished simply, with a muslin curtain draped over a bamboo rod, an old Dutch planter's chair, an earthen pot and a reed mat on the unpolished wooden floor.

ABOVE RIGHT
The bed platform in the center of the attic is covered with mosquito nets. Light filters in under the exposed half-round tiles and timber framework of the roof.

modifications of building methods adopted and perpetuated by the various ethno-cultural groups that have made the island their home through the centuries, in particular rural and urban dwellings and places of worship. Associated with these were travelers' rest buildings and temporary shelters built in the fields during early planting or harvesting, and structures for ritual ceremonies of healing and life-cycle events.

Sri Lankan rural houses developed from the materials from which they were constructed. The simplest houses consisted of *warichchi* walls—a skeleton of jungle wood and bamboo wattle filled with mud—covered with deep overhanging roofs of jungle timber overlaid with plaited coconut fronds or paddy straw thatch (*illuk*). The floors and often parts of the walls were then covered with cow dung to prevent termite attack and to purify the dwelling. The whole style is one of smooth curves that seem both visually and physically molded to accommodate human life, and which also create a soft gradation in light and shade. Doors and windows consisted of large, well-defined members that were shaped with an adze and joined together with timber pins. The door sash itself tended to be of a single plank pivoted on a bottom timber and a top timber, which were a part of the door-frame. The few enclosed rooms were usually used for sleeping by female and younger members of the family, and for storage.

Almost no loose furniture is to be found in these houses, and the high plinths of the verandas that kept out rain and jungle creatures, and the thick half walls that often defined the edges of a veranda served as seating. The occupants invariably slept on the floor on reed mats that were rolled up and hung on loops of coir rope—the *paduru Ana*—from the rafters. The only other possessions were utilitarian items, always beautifully crafted, mostly for kitchen use. Elaborate wooden rice bins were built in the main living space or around the courtyard of many houses. More valuable items and clothes were stored in wooden boxes. Many of these vernacular items are highly sought after as decorative elements by collectors and some feature in the houses in this book.

Shrines and the dwellings of monks and the aristocracy employed the same building principles and materials, except that the exterior walls were often covered with *hunu* lime wash, the exposed woodwork was of much higher quality, and the roof would be covered in flat clay shingles with patterns made visible by the use of a straight-edged and a pointed-

edged tile. In most rural temples, the woodwork takes on a high level of craftsmanship, which reached its apogee in the great royal temples. The interiors are brilliantly painted with stories illustrating moral and spiritual life, the main means of instruction. In both the Hindu and Buddhist faith, where devotion is a personal issue, there is no organized worship, thus the interior, devoid of any furniture, often had either a smooth cow dung floor or terracotta or granite tiles to sit or kneel on for personal devotion in any chosen corner of the shrine. Movable furniture is absent except for perhaps an elaborate table that would be used to place flowers, lamps and incense before the deity. Preceding the entrance of most shrines was an open pavilion, which was the principle place of devotion, and also the drumming hall where the offering of sound was made to the deity being worshipped and concurrently announced the times of worship. Early Islamic mosques followed the pattern of the open pavilion preceded by a courtyard for ablutions. The large pitched roof of the main hall of worship was not unlike a drumming hall of a Buddhist or Hindu shrine. These open pavilions, along with the verandas in dwellings and the wayside resting pavilions, epitomize the essence of outdoor tropical living where the only purpose of buildings was to provide shelter from direct sunlight or torrential rain. The Magul Maduw (Hall of Public Audience) in the historic capital of Kandy is one such open pavilion, where no skill or expense was spared to make it suitable for its purpose as the place of the royal presence.

Temporary structures for various purposes are an integral part of Sri Lankan life. Given that most dwellings are traditionally rather small, any ceremony such as a wedding or ritual healing ceremony demanded that a temporary *maduwa* be erected and decorated with coconut fronds and other leaves. Guests to the royal court in medieval times were accommodated in elaborate versions of these pavilions. Major Davy describes the accommodations that were provided for them by the King of Kandy on their visits to that city in 1802: "These became the precursors under Dutch rule of the rest houses for travellers that are found in the outlying provinces of the island."

The building materials of early urban houses were also more permanent, with rocks and mud replacing wattle and daub, and the exteriors almost universally lime-washed or covered with *samara*. A greater concern with individual privacy resulted in many more sleeping rooms, and the stratification of society

was reflected in the separation of activities such as sleeping, entertaining and cooking. During the early twentieth century, vernacular houses began to show European influences in the incorporation of columns and doors. Turned *beeralu* wooden columns or Tuscan brick piers were used to support veranda roofs. Windows and doors with glass and timber shutters also contained what were very clearly European decorative motifs. The austerity of early Dutch and Portuguese architecture gave way to eclectic Baroque and high Victorian frivolity. Tuscan piers with plain walls gave way to Gothic arches and elaborate pargetted walls. Straightforward eaves of layered tiles gave way to fretwork valance boards with highly elaborate encrustations. Only the steep pitched roof remained, raised even higher by the Dutch to allow for cooler interiors. The floors were almost always made of large terracotta tiles set in lime plaster with highly polished plain or pigmented cement, that were cool to the feet.

As the nineteenth century progressed, rural Sri Lanka homes began to imitate the styles of urban dwellings. This was partly because people sought to imitate what were seen to be more sophisticated styles and partly because the same craftsmen worked in both spheres. By the end of the century this hybrid style was very much in evidence in the vernacular architecture of Sri Lanka, particularly in the coastal regions.

Similar developments occurred in the design of interiors and furniture. Many commonplace items of furniture today were first introduced to Sri Lanka in the sixteenth century by the Portuguese. This is evident in the various terms used for them in the local languages: *mesa*, *almariya*, *janelaya*. The first chairs introduced by the Portuguese incorporated elaborate Sri Lankan carvings. Dutch furniture was much heavier, with large chairs and elaborate four-poster beds being common. Heavy dowry boxes to store linen and other household goods are very much of what is now perceived as Sri Lankan.

Galle Fort Hotel

GALLE FORT | ARCHITECT: CHANNA DASWATTE

A row of tall louvered panels set between white Tuscan columns in Church Street, fast becoming the most fashionable street in the old fort city of Galle, marks the Galle Fort Hotel. Created from the old town mansion of a wealthy family with links to the jewelry business, its most recent incarnation was as a jewelry factory. When the present owners bought the building, it was a warren of partitioned rooms with a courtyard full of temporary buildings made of sheets of corrugated metal and cement blocks forming furnaces for melting the metal to make the jewelry. Since then, driven by the passion that comes from truly falling in love with a place, and a very good eye for detail—and with a little help from an itinerant architect—the building has been transformed into a place with immense charm, one that reveals its own history and the eclectic tastes of its owners.

The classic Dutch-period town house plan was adapted in the conversion of the mansion to a hotel. The veranda, originally wide open to passersby in the street in front, was enclosed on either side with pivoted louvered panels. The louvers not only provide the right amount of privacy for diners in the veranda café, but allow sunshine to stream in through the gaps, producing a delightful play of light. The main hall was opened up and restored to its original glory, complete with its high kitsch archway reputedly designed by the Comte de Mauny of Taprobane Island fame. The two rooms on either side of the hall serve as a bar and a stylish dining room. A large hall beyond forms the main lounge of the hotel. In all these rooms, glass skylights allow the sun to stream on to the walls, an effect that was inspired by the holes in the roof in the original dilapidated building.

ABOVE
Columns and louvers mark the front of the Galle Fort Hotel. The café on the veranda opens out directly to the street. A small board on one of the columns displays the daily menu.

RIGHT
Classic Dutch-period cabinets and tables, 1930s-style armchairs and replicas of nineteenth-century sofas complement the honey-colored walls and floor in the main hall, entered via the original ornate doorway. Soft light from the skylights washes the walls from gaps left in the ceiling panels.

The hall opens on to a terrace at the back of the house and the breathtaking sight of the 25 foot (7.5 meter) high colonnade, which composes one of the wings of the house. Possibly added during an early twentieth-century renovation, the oversized columns support a small upper story that in proportion looks more like an attic but is indeed "Le Grande Suite de la Comte de Mauny"—the most expensive room in the hotel and arguably the largest hotel suite in Sri Lanka.

Some of the other rooms in the hotel take their names from the style in which they have been refurbished. The grand two-level Admiral Cheng Ho Suite, named after the Chinese admiral who visited Dondra Head in 1406, is decorated with Chinese heirloom furniture. The aptly named Portuguese Barracks Suite features a double bath in the bedroom! A new wing of rooms has been added to balance the existing ones and provide additional accommodation, along with a pool in the central courtyard.

ABOVE
The library, filled at one end with comfortable sofas and poufs, is an ideal retreat for a quiet read. Light for reading comes in through the open widnows, shuttered at night. A stunning antique shop display case holds books. The old jackwood floor is covered with coconut fiber rugs, their colors complementing the tones of the floor, walls and ceiling. The small miniature paintings on the walls depict vignettes of Sri Lankan life.

LEFT
The entrance to the library is a modern reproduction inspired by an original door from another house in the Galle Fort. The arch is typical seventeenth century.

RIGHT
The other end of the library is simply furnished with an elegant nineteenth-century table and chairs. Coconut fiber rugs cover the entire length of the jackwood floor.

BELOW
The Grande Suite de la Comte de Mauny on the upper floor of the north-west wing comprises a lounge, shown here, and two bedrooms. The suite is named after the famous count who built Taprobane Island and also reputedly made the early twentieth-century additions to the house. However, the style of the building's interiors is decidedly Georgian.

LEFT
The rooms in the new west wing in the inner courtyard follow the spirit of the existing buildings. The bedrooms open directly on to the timber floored balcony on the upper floor and the pool terrace on the lower floor. The tall verandas offer a pace of life now to be found only in such courtyards as these.

ABOVE
The exaggerated colonnades of the northeast wing are an early twentieth-century eccentricity on eighteenth-century foundations.

RIGHT AND FAR RIGHT
Old jackwood flooring glows in the morning sun. Chinese pomegranates sit on a Sri Lankan brass monk's food stand on a nineteenth-century jackwood *pettagama* or storage box. The modern china is made in Sri Lankan.

LEFT
A nineteenth-century oil press made of granite forms a centerpiece in the forecourt of the small house. The activities of the household, including alfresco dining, can spread out on to the gravel yard. From here, also, the occupants can enjoy the early light that picks up the mist rising from the lake and the marsh garden beyond.

No. 87

BENTOTA | ARCHITECT: GEOFFREY BAWA

No. 87, Galle Road, Bentota, was once a shop house facing the main road. It stood across the road from another elegant two-story shop house of the same late eighteenth-century vintage. Both were rescued from almost certain demolition and oblivion by Lydia Duchini Gunasekera, an Italian sculptor. Together with Geoffrey Bawa, the renowned architect whom she had met when he commissioned a sculpture of a bishop to adorn the ground level of his classroom block at Bishop's College in Colombo, she set out on a mission to rescue the beautiful houses.

No. 87 was bought, along with the land behind it leading to the edge of a large marsh. The house opposite was also bought, but carefully demolished and the salvaged material used to reassemble the building at No. 87, but close to the Galle Road. The single-story shop house was then turned in on the property and a large pavilion added to house the artist's studio, garages and staff quarters. Having been through several incarnations with different owners, the present owner has lovingly restored the buildings, housing within them an exceptional collection of artifacts, and also added a marsh garden. He and his family now use No. 87 as an occasional weekend retreat.

A long painted wall on the main road to Galle marks No. 87. Dark blue and white gates open on to a heavily planted and shaded entrance court. The open pavilion at the entrance is part garage, part dining area. At the far end is the artist's studio and a small elegantly furnished bar. From here the rest of the buildings are revealed, centered around an old tamarind tree on the expansive lawn. The two-story building across the lawn contains two bedrooms and a sitting room on the ground floor with a gallery of early photographs by Sri Lankan Lionel Wendt.

The second house sitting up against the Galle Road also contains two bedrooms, but is also the formal dining area. A small kitchen and pantry are attached and become a barrier between the main living spaces and the noise emanating from the Galle Road.

Both houses are exquisitely reassembled from old parts, with the exception of the large expanses of glass in the wall spaces between the doors and windows. The ancient timber doors and windows are set in glass to allow the houses to be better lit. Everywhere there is meticulous attention to detail in the restoration. At the far end, the lawn ends in an open vista over a large lake and an expansive garden fashioned out of the surrounding marsh.

Antique columns on the veranda of the small house frame a peaceful, monochromatic garden bathed in late afternoon light.

The single-story house is framed by two huge breadfruit trees (*Artocarpus incisa*). The white walls stand in stark contrast to the gray shingled roof, the stained wood window shutters and the green surroundings.

A seventeenth-century door framed in glass in the two-story second house is an ideal place from which to view the marsh garden in the distance through an antique brass telescope.

LEFT
Morning light streams in through an upper floor window in the second house to light up ancient floor boards, a weathered nineteenth-century timber bench and three framed photographs taken in 1935 by famed Sri Lankan photographer Lionel Wendt. The white walls form a neutral canvas for the play of light and shadow.

The Dutch House

GALLE | ARCHITECT: CHANNA DASWATTE

The Dutch House in Galle is part of a chain of bungalows that have been converted into stylish inns along the south coast of Sri Lanka. Originally built as Doorenberg ("Thorn Hill") in 1712 during the period of Dutch East India Company administration, the house may have served as a retirement residence or country seat for an important official. From the front of the house, there are breathtaking views of the old fort of the Galle Commadant and the sea beyond.

The owner, who already had a guest house on upper Dickson Road across from Doorenberg, had always admired the crumbling old house that was for a long time an orphanage run by the Anglican Church. With all the orphans grown up and gone, the place was barely inhabited and in a dilapidated state. A proposition was made to the local church authorities, agreement reached, and Doorenberg was then beautifully restored to its

present condition. In the restoration, period features of Sri Lankan architecture were considered along with a healthy respect for the almost Palladian proportions of the house. Ill-advised additions and partitions made over the years were pulled down and the grand proportions of the house revealed. An additional wing, now called The Ballroom, was added, in the process creating a semi-enclosed courtyard looking out over a croquet lawn. A small swimming pool was also added, but over the edge of the hill among the trees, behind a stand of royal palms bordering the garden of the neighboring manor house.

Doorenberg is now approached via a forecourt of red gravel and a low wall, which reveals the magnificent view of the old town in the distance and provides a fitting foreground to the simple and austere façade. A hedge of white hibiscus forms a screen to the private gardens of the suites. The sparely

RIGHT
A low cement wall borders the red gravel driveway to the house, here graced by an early twentieth-century Rover convertible. The fort can be seen in the distance through the trees.

BELOW
The Ballroom suite, so-called because of its lofty proportions, is a modern addition, but built along the same lines as the original old house. Dutch-period doors and windows, salvaged from demolition sites, and Dutch furniture give a period feel to the suite. Polished cement tiles echo the pattern of the terracotta tiles found in the original house, which were discovered upon excavation but were unusable due to years of neglect and chipping when subsequent floors were laid.

RIGHT
Crisp cotton contrasts with soft linen in this bedroom. The four-poster bed is of a seventeenth-century Indo-Portuguese design from Sri Lanka's Portuguese colonial period. The high bed head and end and the turned wooden spindles are peculiar to the furniture of the time and were a mark of fine craftsmanship. A comfortable sitting area adjoins the bedroom.

BELOW
A similar four-poster bed dominates the bedroom of the Ballroom Suite. Trade cloth hangings from the nineteenth century flank the door separating the bedroom from the bathroom beyond. The oche palette is carried throughout the house as are the polished pigmented floor tiles which were based on the originals.

Light throws the curved forms into silhouette and bathes the bathroom of the Ballroom Suite. The pigmented cement finished surfaces glow with a welcoming warmth.

furnished veranda leads into the hallway with its seventeenth-century chairs and locally made brass chandelier, a copy of one hanging in the old town hall in Cape Town.

The ambience of the interior has been achieved through a clever mix of colonial furniture and practical modern designs. The muted palette of ochre, derived from traditional wall finishes such as *samara* and lime wash, and the faded yellow polished cement floor tiles give this house a truly peaceful feel.

Each room in the house has a different color scheme, inspired by paintings by the old Dutch masters. The great silk full-height curtains in the bedrooms add operatic grandeur befitting the proportions of the house. Old prints and modern paintings hang side by side in all of the rooms.

Arriving guests are greeted by the all-female resident staff and treated with all the care and attention reminiscent of a visit to a grandmother's house!

LEFT
In the bathroom in the Eastern Suite, a modern polished cement vanity top inset with cement basins is juxtaposed with an antique bathtub on claw legs. A typically Dutch curved wall at the far end conceals the shower and toilet. An unusual feature in the bathroom is the window seat, which allows the bather—or a companion— views of the garden or a place to sit and chat.

RIGHT
The living room of the Western or Blue Suite opens out to the garden. A copy of an eighteenth-century Wolfendahal chair (named after the church in Colombo where they were used as pews) sits in front of a British-period console that doubles as a writing desk. A colonial-period chaise longue, covered in blue fabric, makes for comfortable lounging.

Mudannayake House

COLOMBO 7 | ARCHITECT: UNKNOWN

The Colombo suburb of Cinnamon Gardens was once a leafy paradise of low, creeper-clad walls and generously sized gardens. Few of the houses in the area have, however, survived the onslaught of modern political and economic pressures. Those that have are most likely to be occupied by an embassy or be the residence of a high-ranking diplomat. Among the most beautiful of all is the Prime Minister's office on Flower Road. Also on Flower Road is the Mudannayake house, one which is still lived in by a family in the great tradition of British colonial houses in Sri Lanka. Built in the early part of the twentieth century, the house exemplifies the eclectic classical style which developed in the tropical colonies. It has large verandas with seemingly Ionic columns but the architecture is, in fact, an amalgam of colonial and local architectural traditions and influences.

The entrance to the formally designed house is defined by a large porte-cochere and a veranda bordered by large, gleaming white Tuscan columns and balustrates. Dark-stained doors open off the veranda to a grand central hallway, which forms the main reception areas, demarcated by more white columns. Beyond the central hallway, a staircase leads to the upper floor. Cool marble floors composed of large white slabs intersected at the corners with small black squares form a continuous surface from the veranda right throughout the reception areas. White painted walls and high ceilings add further to the open, spacious feel of the ground floor of the house.

The upper floor houses most of the private spaces, such as bedrooms, although a veranda overlooking the terrace over the porte-cochere is used as a dining area. This space captures the essence of tropical living, with breezes

ABOVE
The symmetrical Ionic columned porte-cochere is typical of the grand houses of the nineteenth century that lined the shaded avenues of the elegant Cinnamon Gardens suburb of Colombo.

RIGHT
The ground-floor veranda is furnished with reclining wooden chairs and white-painted cane furniture—both ubiquitous colonial accouterments.

from the lush green front garden wafting throughout. All rooms, both upstairs and downstairs, have verandas that provide shade from the sweltering tropical sun and protection from the monsoon rains.

In complete contrast to the house's commanding façade, its bold columns and high ceilings, the furniture is fine and delicate, typical of that favored by the British. The ground-floor entertainment rooms are furnished with classic ebony furniture which is set off to good effect in the whiteness around. Simpler hardwood furniture occupies the rest of the house, with some painted cane furniture on the verandas. Collections of contemporary, mostly Sri Lankan, art adorn the walls and add color to a muted palette.

The whiteness against the lush green, the cool marble floors and sparsely furnished interior epitomize the classic colonial style of the British period. The gracious proportions and simple planning lend colonial houses of this tradition a calm, serene atmosphere.

ABOVE
A table set for a formal dinner party catches the light of the setting sun. The profusion of palm trees and other tropical vegetation outside forms a magical backdrop.

LEFT
The marble-floored veranda at the entrance to the house is sparsely furnished with nineteenth-century style wooden chairs and white-painted cane furniture. The lush vegetation surrounding the veranda provides a cool contrast to the white building which sparkles in the bright sunshine.

RIGHT
Pink-hued terrazzo walls and floors are a perfect backdrop for a free-standing green enamel bathtub. The elaborate gilt-painted legs and brass taps add a touch of luxury.

BELOW
The reception rooms are both spacious and gracefully appointed. Heirloom ebony furniture, softly lit by the glow of crystal chandeliers, helps to create an old-world charm. Potted palms and ceiling fans add to the colonial air, while marble floors contribute to the timeless quality of the rooms. The pot in the foreground is a fine example of seventeenth century kitchenware exported from China and found in all centers along the sea trade routes.

Horagolla Stables

NITTAMBUWA | ARCHITECT: GEOFFREY BAWA

The outward appearance of the stables at the old manor house at Horagolla on Kandy Road is one of a well-proportioned and elegant classical manor. Originally built to house the six thoroughbred horses of one of the highest native officials of the land under the British colonial administration, Sir Solomon Bandaranaike, whose family went on to dominate national politics for the better part of post-independence Sri Lanka, the original buildings were built on a grand scale, with a hayloft and quarters for grooms and others who looked after the animals. Politics obviously did not leave the family much time for riding and the old stables fell into disrepair. The magnificent building was saved in the nick of time by Sir Soloman's only grandchild not involved in politics. With the help of architect Geoffrey Bawa, she carefully restored and converted the old stables into a weekend retreat.

In the process of transformation, Bawa added a porch in the same design as the rest of the house with a bedroom above, and a

ABOVE
A charming pavilion in the western garden marks the central axis of the house. Although newly added to the house, it is composed of four old columns and a door salvaged from an eighteenth-century Dutch-period house.

LEFT
The oculus at the end of the entrance veranda focuses the attention on the axial quality of the space.

RIGHT
An old clay pot used for salting fish makes a bold statement on a low table made from a single plank of *para mara* (*Samanea saman*). Polished cement floors provide a neutral backdrop in the original stall area, now the main living room.

ABOVE
A small painted image
of the Buddha from the
Kandy period, surrounded
by a stylized halo, is one
of the many artifacts from
this period that are part
of the art collection in the
living room and veranda.

RIGHT
The old horse stalls, still
labeled with the names of
their former occupants,
form the main living room
of the converted stables.
Clusters of comfortable
sofas and armchairs on
the ground floor and in the
former hayloft are inter-
spersed with well-chosen
antiques. In the sitting area
here, a modern upholstered
sofa is surrounded by
black and white cane chairs.
Above, leather butterfly
chairs are casually arranged
in front of a painting by
Saskia Pingiers, flanked by
a pair of satinwood and
ebony cupboards.

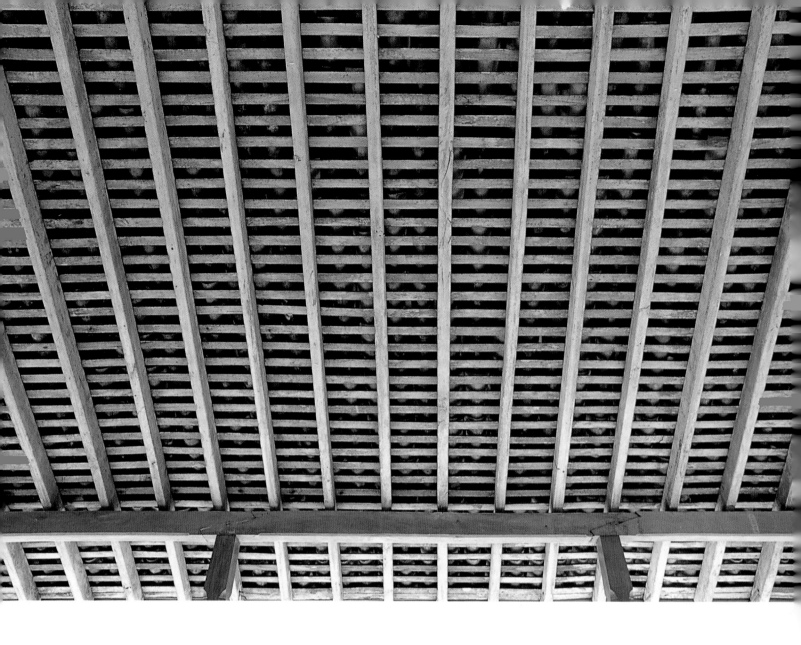

ABOVE
The half-round terracotta tiles that cover the veranda are visible through the gaps in the traditional timber frame roof.

RIGHT
A painted panel, part of a nineteenth-century temple ceiling in the tradition of the Kandyan school of painting, hangs over a sofa in the main veranda. The colors and style of the painting, which depicts a narrative of one of the birth stories of Buddha, are typical of the period.

service wing, which also contained an additional bedroom. The house is now approached
through the gardens of the old house along
a narrow and chicaned carriageway bordered
by hibiscus. The main entrance under the
porch leads into a hallway with a low roof,
lined with rubbings of the famous *gal potha*
or stone book in the sacred rectangle at
Polonnaruwa, and then on into the main part
of the house. A small stairway off the hallway
leads to a guest room over the entrance.

Beyond the main house, a veranda wraps
around two sides of an impeccably kept lawn.
This unites the old building on the left with
the new wing on the right. The veranda of
the new wing contains a dining area, with a
kitchen and other service areas behind, and
a guest room at one end. The veranda beside
the old wing ends in a circular hole in the
wall matched by another on the porch wall
that sets up the main axis in the house. The
horses' accommodation in the old stable was
converted into a magnificent sitting room,
and the quarters of the stable hands and staff
converted into two grand bedrooms and
bathrooms. A veranda on the other end leads
into a second lawn with a garden pavilion.

LEFT
An eighteenth-century
column, reused in the
garden pavilion on the
western lawn, comes from
a roadside house which,
like many others, has given
way to development.

BELOW
An unusual ceiling panel
from a temple depicting
the Buddha in the compa-
ny of his disciples hangs
over an eighteenth-century
box in the main veranda.
The small bronze sculpture
of Shiva astride his bull
is by local sculptor Tissa
Ranasinghe.

An Artist's Residence

GALLE | ARCHITECT: UNKNOWN

The various colonial periods in Sri Lankan history exerted a tremendous influence not only on civic architecture and the mansions of the colonial masters, but also on the construction of country houses belonging to local gentry, which exhibited many colonial traits along with local traditions. This may well have been deliberate or merely because the builders and masons of the period simply built like that, automatically incorporating a fusion of elements and styles from various periods.

These country houses were almost formulaic in plan, with a colonnaded veranda in front leading to a large central hall bisected by an archway or two and with two or four rooms opening off it. The back of the hall, in turn, opened on to another veranda. The verandas and central hall all had high roofs, and above the hall there was often a timber-boarded attic, which created a ceiling for the hall below and provided the necessary insulation from the heat. A small stairway often led into the attic for use as storage.

ABOVE
The tile-roofed, colonnaded house is almost hidden from view by the wild garden with its profusion of fruit trees, palms and other tropical species.

LEFT
The pavilion amongst the trees is an extension of the attic. The far end is covered in mats made from the talipot palm, providing easy and relaxed seating.

RIGHT
The plain polished cement veranda, with its edge highlighted in white, is a cool oasis in the midst of the surrounding vegetation. The extension, built at right angles to the main axis of the house, is sometimes used for dining.

One such house, located on a wooded hill outside Galle, is occupied by an Italian artist. Set in a "wild" garden, the entrance veranda is bare except for a table for reading or dining placed in an extension to the attic, built at right angles to the house. Another local adaptation, a square Tuscan column with chamfered edges, supports the deep eave and the upper-level extension. The hall is sparsely furnished, accentuating the architecture and the importance of the two arches that separate the space. The original terracotta floor tiles create a warm glow in the otherwise white lime-plastered room. Four rooms open off this space, one with access to the attic. A back veranda supported by simple wooden columns opens out into the rear part of the garden.

The attic and its extension over the veranda act as both studio and meditation space for the artist. Here, the low roof and soft light, the timber-framed roof and exposed half-round tiles contribute to the intimate atmosphere, while the open veranda extension allows for contemplation of the garden from above. The low railings and mats encourage one to sit on the floor, as is the case in most other parts of the house which have minimal formal furniture. The house is mostly adorned with collections of paintings and *objets d'art* rather than functional furniture and domesticity. The décor suggests simplicity of style with nothing but the essentials coming between the enjoyment of the pure and elegant spaces of the old house itself.

ABOVE
The hall is almost empty except for a single chaise longue against the back wall. The old terracotta floor tiles are cool to the feet and are comfortable enough to sit on. Fine muslin curtains over the doorways cut the harsh glare of the sunlight.

ABOVE
A small glass skylight inserted between the half-round roof tiles lights the painted timber staircase leading to the office above.

LEFT
A collection of seashells nestles in an old terracotta curd pot. The framed nineteenth-century post-cards show various views of old Ceylon.

LEFT
The bed platform in the attic, draped with mosquito netting, is strategically placed to enjoy the view along the whole length of the upper-floor veranda. Two painted ceiling planks flank the doorway. A footstool and reed mats are the only other furnishings on the veranda.

RIGHT
The study-studio in the attic is filled with soft, low lighting from both the gaps in the tiles and the low windows. The boarded floor is unpolished. An Indian kilim adds a touch of color to the otherwise neutral tones in the room.

Iluketiya Bungalow

ILUKETIYA | ARCHITECT: CHAN SAU YAN

The hinterland of the south coast of Sri Lanka is an area of tropical verdure away from the hustle and bustle of Galle Road and its ribbon of urban and suburban sprawl. Here, life slows down to a pre-industrial pace.

Overlooking a small lake and paddy fields, and set among tranquil gardens and the cinnamon plantations that are a part of this area, is Iluketiya, a bungalow inspired by the simple dwellings of the small-scale farmers who own and work the land. Although the bungalow is new, it draws its inspiration from several indigenous forms, but also resolves some of the problems that these houses often have, such as poor interior lighting and the lack of open large spaces that are today considered necessary for modern living.

The materials used in constructing the house include traditional plastered brick walls painted white on the inside and ochre on the outside. Half-round tiles sit exposed on the rafters in the verandas and outside areas, but are hidden by simple timber plank ceilings in the interior. Extensive use has been made of old doors and windows salvaged from late nineteenth- and early twentieth-century Sri Lanka houses. The house is also filled with numerous antiques, art and artifacts from various parts of Asia.

Central to life in Iluketiya is a large, formal sitting room filled with an exotic collection of sturdy bamboo furniture from Linda Garland in Bali, Chinese tapered cabinets, modern steel coffee tables and quirky chandeliers. A Balinese painting fills the end wall. Flooded with natural light, the room opens on three sides to the tiled, colonnaded verandas that surround it and to profusely planted gardens and long pools filled with lotuses and other water plants. Perforated wooden panels above the paneled doors and

RIGHT
Stone steps lead to moat-like pools surrounding the living pavilion. Deep verandas and eaves and surrounding vegetation, together with the water, provide relief from the intense tropical heat. A brilliant bougainvillea adds a splash of color.

the high roof not only provide decoration but also allow natural ventilation and reduce glare, making the house remarkably cool in the tropical heat. Groups of chairs on the veranda—as well as the stone steps leading down to the ponds—provide ample seating for the occupants and their visitors.

The fourth (rear) side of the living room opens on to a courtyard, which links it to the rest of the living quarters and the service areas of the house. Inspired by a traditional courtyard, this one, however, is filled with water, with the soothing sound of water trickling from an overflowing pot, its reflection adding beauty to the pool. Bedrooms surround this courtyard. All the bedrooms, furnished with the minimum of furniture, also open on to private views of the surrounding gardens. Large doors and windows let in the scents and sounds of the tropics.

At the far end of the courtyard, a two-story entertainment annex opens up with a double-height vestibule leading to an attic reached by a wooden staircase. The attic comprises a spacious sitting room opening out to a veranda, and an adjoining library and billiards room. The sitting area is furnished with a stunning Afghan carpet and floor cushions covered in handwoven Baluchi rugs in bright tones of fuchsia and pink, heightening the brilliance of the light spilling in through the stained-glass window on the gable end of the room. The built-in seating on the adjoining veranda is similarly furnished in pink. The billiards room off the main seating area is more formally appointed. Chairs for watching play in progress line the walls surrounding the central table. Both rooms, however, boast the same beautiful views of the garden and countryside.

LEFT
Antique timber columns frame the greenery beyond this informal veranda off the annex sitting room. The terracotta objects on the ledge are contemporary Sri Lankan work based on ancient designs. The white cement floor provides an effective contrast between inside and out.

LEFT
A stone-floored double-height vestibule is the entry point to the annex to the main house. The wooden stairs, which are also from an old house, lead to the light-filled attic and the library and billiards room beyond.

BELOW LEFT
The attic leading to the library and billiards room is an informal sitting area. The floor cushions, made from a collection of Baluchi rugs, complement the Afghan carpet.

LEFT
Sunlight streams into the billiards room on the upper floor. The windows are recycled from an early twentieth-century colonial house. The ventilation grilles of Victorian inspiration were very much a part of the Sri Lankan architectural traditions of the period. The chairs and table are from the same period. Terracotta ventilation roof tiles make unusual light fittings on the wall.

BELOW
The calm, quiet courtyard at the back of the house derives from a long Sri Lankan architectural tradition, but is here filled with water. The edge is made from a collection of old items as are the doors and columns. The warm yellow polished terracotta walls have been painted with traditional *samara* paint. The glazed terracotta pot was part of the East India Company's trade with the island's ports during the seventeenth century.

The Hill Club

NUWARA ELIYA | ARCHITECT: EDWARDS, REID AND BEGG

Nowhere in Sri Lanka do the vestiges of colonial Britain live on as obviously as in the hill country. The central massif, traditionally left bare of any settlement by the indigenous population, was opened up for the cultivation of, first, coffee and then tea from 1846. In 1860 Samuel Baker "discovered" the high valley of Nuwara Eliya and established a farm in it. Many colonials, drawn by the healthier, almost English climate that allowed for a lifestyle much akin to that of their distant homeland, and Nuwara Eliya ("New-ralia" to the British, or "Little England" as it is aptly referred to), came to resemble a little village from the home counties of England. The plantation houses and holiday homes of those who flocked to the hills during the warmest pre-monsoon months, including the governors of the day, stand to this day amidst pictur-esque gardens full of sweet peas and gladioli,

shielded from the high winds by stands of Monterey cypress and eucalyptus trees.

By 1876 a club, that essential institution of British life, was founded and aptly called the Hill Club, and by 1896 the second oldest golf club outside the British Isles was estab-lished in the valley. Although much of the area's charm has now disappeared under post-colonial settlement and vegetable cultivation, the core of the town in and around the Golf Club and the key institutions of the Hill Club, Golf Club, St Andrew's Hotel and Grand Hotel still remain as British as they were when first established. The faded elegance of the Hill Club and Golf Club, with their tradition-al fare of cheese toast and tea, epitomize the quintessential colonial style of Sri Lanka.

The present Hill Club building dates from the 1930s when it was built by the British, Colombo-based firm of Edwards, Reid and

ABOVE
Portraits of Queen Eliza-beth II and Prince Philip and the Prince and Prin-cess of Wales flank that of the president of Sri Lanka and patron of the club in the heavy-beamed reading room. The faux leather upholstered chairs are based on a nineteenth-century design. The maga-zine rack and newspaper stand are late Victorian.

LEFT
The Scottish baronial-style Hill Club was built in the 1930s by the colonial architectural firm of Edwards, Reid and Begg. Locally sourced stone and fake timbering lend appropriate dignity to the club.

BELOW
Chintz-covered sofas and armchairs and gilt-framed pictures provide the reassurance of a home county living room.

OVERLEAF
Starched white, brass-buttoned jackets and crisp white sarongs are the uniform for the stewards in the high-beamed dining room. Furnished with basic utilitarian nineteenth-century colonial chairs, comfort above beauty was more important in the club. The room is lent an air of sophistication by the immaculate white table linen and candles. It is still *de rigueur* for men to wear a tie and jacket at dinner.

Begg in a Scottish baronial style in local dressed granite. Its imposing presence is enhanced by its location on a hill overlooking the golf course and its own expansive lawns, bordered by flower beds and scattered with umbrella-shaded tables and chairs where one can enjoy an English afternoon tea.

The interior of the Hill Club is an eclectic mixture of practical furnishings surviving from the different periods of its existence, together with the trappings associated with the British hill station lifestyle: fireplaces, mounted hunting trophies, framed portraits and scenes and vases of temperate flowers. The dark wood of the floors and furniture contribute to the club's grand appearance.

The stone porch in front of the club leads into a large hallway. The men's bar opens directly off this space, as does the library. These are distinctly masculine spaces originally meant for the all-male club—only in the twentieth century were ladies allowed into the club through the main entrance. A long corridor at the far side of the entrance hall connects the other spaces, including the billiards room, dining room and lounge.

A fishing trophy (above) from the time when the streams and lakes around Nuwara Eliya were well stocked with rainbow trout introduced by the British in the nineteenth century. Old aerated water bottles (below) adorn a self in the dining room.

ABOVE
Red oxide floors contrast with the green baize of the nineteenth-century billiard table and the basic teak furniture. The white ceiling with painted copper panels is common in many colonial buildings in the hill country.

LEFT
Sturdy teak beds complete with feather duvets and hot water bottles welcome guests in the spacious bedrooms. The beds and scroll-legged side tables are all of late nineteenth-century British colonial design. The teak floorboards are covered with a well-worn carpet.

LEFT
The skull and horns of
an Axis deer adorning
the wall does double duty
as a coat hook.

Galapita

BUTTALA | ARCHITECT: RUKMAN FONSEKA

The southeastern corner of Sri Lanka is linked to the sacred site of Kataragama, the abode of Sri Skanda, the God of War, and a classic pilgrimage shrine, second only to that of the Scared Mountain of Adam's Peak. The area is linked with remoteness and mystery associated with the god and his dalliances with a local Veddah maiden, Valli Amman. Here, the last vestiges of a pastoral and a hunter-gatherer culture still survive amidst the magnificent backdrop of the southern foothills and the plains that lead to the east coast. Here also, this far-flung corner of the island has, through its sheer inaccessibility, been spared the often unforgiving ravages of development.

A little way up the Menik Ganga, the river on which Sri Skanda's shrine is founded, is an island reached via a rope bridge across the rocky ravine of the swiftly flowing river (swift, at least, during the monsoon). On one side of the island the river emerges as a placid, tranquil and shallow, stone-bottomed stream shaded by massive *kumbuk* (*Terminalia arjuna*) trees. Beyond, on top of the island's rocks stands Galapita, literally "on top of the rock," a highly original "natural" retreat.

A series of simple open pavilions are built on and around the rocks on the island using the traditional methods of wattle-and-daub construction. On the highest part is the sleeping pavilion. Mud platform steps go down the slope of the rock, allowing different levels on which to sleep, usually on thin mattresses laid on reed mats. On the lowest level, an antique four-poster bed under a high roof gives the impression of sleeping outside.

The dining pavilion is set on the ground level using part of the high rock as a sheltering wall, but otherwise is totally open to the elements. On the upper part of this pavilion, on level with the sleeping area on the rock, is another special sleeping space reached by a rustic stepladder. Here, bamboo and coconut *ekel* blinds provide privacy in a space that is otherwise totally open to the sky. A similar sleeping area is made in a traditional tree house pavilion in the paddy fields surrounding the property on the banks of the river. Bathrooms and toilets are set apart from the main living areas behind stone walls for privacy. The outdoor shower spouts make bathing under the canopy of leaves a natural and romantic experience.

ABOVE
An elephant *vahanam* of the God Vibhishan or Saman stands guard at an entrance. These wooden animals were used as part of the ritual of Hindu temples in which images of the gods were taken in procession atop their respective mounts.

RIGHT
A driftwood table is the centerpiece of the main sitting area, a wonderful setting for resting, talking and savoring nature. Mud and cow dung floors, molded into platforms for seating and covered with mats and colorful cushions, meld with the surrounding landscape, making it hard to distinguish between interior and exterior. The old Dutch planters' chairs add a touch of luxury!

ABOVE
A hand-molded goddess stands sentinel at the entrance to this sleeping pavilion overlooking the swift-flowing river.

LEFT
The main sleeping pavilion consists of mud- and cow dung-plastered platforms covered with talipot palm-leaf mats on which are laid thin cotton mattresses. Hammocks are an option to sleeping on the platform. Mosquito nets, for use when necessary, are suspended from jungle poles, while bamboo and reed blinds can be lowered to form "walls."

RIGHT
The main sleeping pavilion sits atop the rock overlooking the Menik Ganga.

FAR RIGHT
Paddy fields bordering the Menik Ganga contribute to the quiet and tranquil atmosphere of the retreat in this remote southeastern corner of Sri Lanka.

BELOW
The wattle-and-daub kitchen is built in the style of a traditional firewood kitchen, complete with smoke racks for keeping things dry. The rice winnowing trays hanging above the fireplace are used to clean rice and other grains before they are cooked.

Island Eclecticism

"All the world's a stage"
—William Shakespeare

The caravans and ocean vessels of old linked East and West along the interconnected routes of the great land and sea Silk Road. Silks and other precious commodities from China were carried across the deserts and mountains of southern Asia to the markets of Asia Minor, northern Africa and other points, and in exchange artifacts found their way back to China. Arab traders dominated the ocean space, which stretched from southern China to Zanzibar to Batavia, carrying anything from rubies to spices to apes. Sri Lanka, referred to by Arabs as Serendib, occupied the center of this ocean space and functioned as an entrepôt, a place for the exchange of mysterious goods and mystic ideas, a place where Arab and Chinese boats met.

Although these exchanges were significant for the development and flowering of the great civilizations of the world, as well as for laying the foundations of our modern world, no other age has been more synonymous with the exchange and availability of ideas and information than the late twentieth century. Global communications, coupled with the ability to transport goods with ease across great distances, have created a culture that is sometimes hard to distinguish by its geographical location alone. This is particularly apparent in the global style in interiors and living styles that prevail around the world. Sri Lanka has not escaped this global thrust, and at various stages of its stylistic development, eclecticism has come into play in the

PREVIOUS PAGE
Striking silhouettes of Galle Fort from the Cinnamon House (page 92).

ABOVE
A colorful collection of cushions covered in hand-loom fabric from Barefoot makes a lively setting for a blue glass Indian candle stand in the Galle Face Court Dome (page 74).

RIGHT
A marble bust sits on an eighteenth-century jack-wood *almirah* made from single planks of wood in the dining room of the Cinnamon House (page 92). The base of the bust is turned coconut wood.

LEFT
Long poles draped with the owner's collection of exotic textiles, among them Indonesian batik, are a focal point on the wall in the master bedroom in the house on 79, Leyn Baan Street (page 98). The bed at the end is built into the wall as a timber platform and hung with a mosquito net.

RIGHT
The perfect circle of the polished cement bathtub in the master bathroom of the Eden House (page 104) is backed by a delicately covered window and two Chinese bamboo ladders used as towel racks. The teak floor forms a "carpet" beneath the tub.

life and style of its people. While a fusion of global influences and their assimilation with traditional styles and attitudes is the cornerstone of Sri Lankan style, the eclecticism that has emerged is different in that it allows the products of various cultures and civilizations to co-exist within the same space, sometimes harmoniously and sometimes discordantly, but always amusingly.

Eclecticism in style derives from exposure to the various cultures of the world, often at first hand, and an appreciation of each object in itself. Each is seen to have its own merit in terms of beauty and enjoyment and is not subservient to another. Tableau are created using various objects, and in the best examples the whole atmosphere celebrates a place or event. Well-traveled and informed individuals create places for relaxation and enjoyment that are global in focus and bring into play numerous ideas and objects that they have seen and gathered that represent their experiences. The world is inspiration and a stage is set for its celebration.

There is, in fact, a long tradition of eclecticism in interiors and architecture in Sri Lanka, stemming partly from its long history of rule by various colonial powers but also from the rise of an affluent middle class under British rule. Success in business and enterprise and the global reach of the empire that included Sri Lanka, then Ceylon, gave rise to a well-traveled group of citizens who returned home with various luxury goods as mementoes of their journeys. These invariably found

a place in their homes. Many mid-century Sri Lankan houses were full of objects from various stylistic and artistic traditions. Art Deco was at home with Victorian and Chinese porcelain. Ivory miniatures sat alongside Lalique glass under Venetian chandeliers lighting up Persian carpets. In architecture, buildings such as Lakshmigiri and College House in Colombo, both built by the De Soysa family, aimed at emulating an eclectic Italianate style inspired by the fancy dress ball of styles then happening in Britain, whilst others copied Oriental or Moorish palaces from their experiences in Andalusia. This innate need to emulate other cultures was also reflected in the clothes people wore and the attitudes they adopted. Photographs in Arnold Wright's monumental *Twentieth Century Impressions of Ceylon* (1907) show pictures of eminent Sri Lankan families amidst the treasures they gathered and in the clothes they wore, witness to their eclectic tastes and experiences.

The current trend towards eclecticism in Sri Lanka stems from the opening of the island's economy in 1977 and the subsequent free flow of ideas and objects. The fact that Sri Lankans travel abroad more frequently and that the country is home to numerous well-traveled expatriates, has also brought about a sea change in the contemporary design styles of interiors. Design stores, too, importing objects of desire for a population exposed to a wide range of ideas and thoughts through the media, have also contributed to changing attitudes in design and lifestyle.

LEFT
Late afternoon sun streams
into the sparse main living
space with its minimal
built-in furniture. A specially woven rush mat creates
softness underfoot and
provides a warm ambience
in the mostly white room.

RIGHT
The imposing Art Deco
entrance staircase leading
up to the tented dome,
its teak railings curving
down to the floor, confers
a striking sense of entry.

Galle Face Court Dome

COLOMBO 3 | ARCHITECT: EDWARDS, REID AND BEGG

The dome of the Galle Face Court Apartment enjoys one of the most stunning settings
of any residence in Colombo. Located on the
southeastern corner of the main public space
of the city, it is not for the weak-hearted. The
magnificent saucer dome, inspired perhaps
by Hagia Sophia itself, has an almost sacred
presence, the repository of some high-powered
relic. Perhaps it is for this reason that it was
occupied for years only by the workshop of
a jeweler until the present occupant convinced
the owners of the apartment building to lease
the space to him. The process took time, but
eventually the craftsman moved out.

The residence comprises simply the circular room under the saucer-shaped dome of the
stunning Art Deco building built by the firm
Edwards, Reid and Begg in 1934. Approached from the elevator hall below, the first sight
of the inside of the dome is nothing short
of breathtaking. The original white smooth-
finished surface has been given a fabric tent.
More recently, the tent has given way to light
projections of images on to it, creating a stunning effect. With the polished white cement
floors there is a feeling of lightness and freedom. The rails of the curved stairs bend down
to the floor as if in homage to the space!

ABOVE
The kitchen is sandwiched between two pillar extensions, its built-in polished terrazzo countertop and teak-stripped cupboards adding style and color to the arc. A dining table is built on the end of one of the extensions.

RIGHT
The saucer-shaped dome from the bedroom terrace.

Behind the grand staircase, with its sturdy teak railings, an imposing wooden mask takes pride of place in a niche. In the round interior, the dome's supporting pillars demarcate certain functions. Minor extensions to the pillars have created a niche for the library on one side of the staircase and, adjoining it, a small, arc-shaped kitchen appointed in wood. A built-in sofa between two pillars takes up another side of the space. The rest of the main space, which is dominated by a large circular rush mat, a red-lacquered Chinese cabinet and a platform bed, serves a variety of functions: as sitting room, dining room, guest room, or simply a relaxing place to lounge.

To the left of the stairway, and up a few steps, is a small bedroom and bathroom that have been built on the adjoining roof terrace. A platform bed, a small table to work at a computer, a cupboard and a ladder placed against a wall to hang sarongs make up the furniture. This apartment is any person's dream location and space, but to live in it requires a rare eclectic skill!

RIGHT
Late evening sun paints
a wall in the bedroom in
several shades of color.

FAR RIGHT
The tented ceiling soars
up to the apex of the main
space.

BELOW
The spare bedroom is an
extension on an adjoining
roof terrace. The owner's
collection of sarongs is
draped on a bamboo lad-
der. A small workspace is
created with a nineteenth-
century colonial table and
an antique Chinese horse-
shoe back chair. Simple
cement cubes form handy
bedside tables.

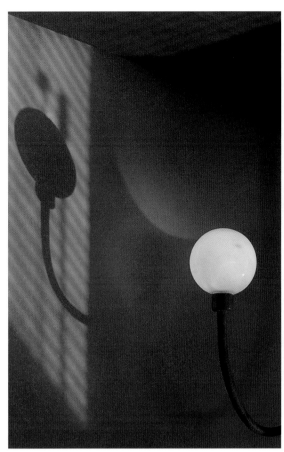

The specially made rush mat dominates the center of the dome. Adding touches of color are bright blue cushions on the built-in sofa and a handsome Chinese red-lacquered cabinet with a bold brass lock. Artifacts from various parts of Asia adorn the top of the cupboard and pillar extension.

Lighthouse Street House

GALLE FORT | ARCHITECT: RANJAN ALUVIHARE

Like many other houses in the city of Galle, No. 41 is at its core a modest house built during the eighteenth-century Dutch period when the city was for almost a hundred years the capital of the Galle Commandant, or the southern province of the Dutch possessions of what was then Ceylon. Modified over time, particularly in the nineteenth century, the most recent renovations have been done to create a second home for a young bachelor who required a place to "chill out" with his friends. The core of the original house has been converted into the main reception room and an entirely new building has been added where the old dilapidated staff and service wing used to be, to house the bedrooms.

Entrance to the house, deceptively modest from the outside, is via a black-and-white tiled veranda enclosed by a low wall set with swing gates. On the wall is a series of timber columns supporting both the roof and a simple latticework screen that helps cut out the evening sun and the prying eyes of passersby. From the plain, but unusual front doors, a colonnaded entrance hall leads to the formal sitting and dining room and the patio and swimming pool in the inner court. Early wrought-iron grilles below timber-lined skylights cast shadows on the black-and-white tiled floors of the entrance hall, lit at night by an old carriage lamp. To the left of the entrance hall, through the colonnade, in what would have originally been one of two front bedrooms is a billiards room and bar, and to the right a quiet room for meditation. The original *zaal*, the long room facing the courtyard, is used on the left end as a sitting room and on the right as a dining room.

The main living space is, however, the courtyard on which most of the attention in the renovation was lavished. A large swimming pool is the centrepiece of this space. The pool occupies most of the yard except for a small area at the far end, next to the house, where

RIGHT
Late evening light reflects off the pool, enhancing the water theme of the courtyard and the honey color of the timber columns. The latticework theme of the front entrance is carried through to the windows and doors in the new wing.

ABOVE
The grilled skylights above the entrance hall offset the cool dark spaces around them. The checkered floor and archways evoke nostalgic images of times gone by.

LEFT
The billiards room and bar, off the entrance hall, are part of the old structure and are in the front of the house. A mirrored alcove helps to create an illusion of space in this otherwise small room. The black-and-white tiled floor is a continuation of the entrance hall.

RIGHT
A view of the hallway from the front door through to the courtyard at the back.

FAR RIGHT
Late afternoon light casts interesting patterns on the walls of the narrow outer veranda. The latticework screens between the veranda posts afford transparency as well as privacy. The distressed blue paint on the latticework and the nineteenth-century louver shutters—still in working condition—was inspired by a color often found on colonial roadside houses.

BELOW
The meditation room at the front of the house is sparsely furnished with simple wood furniture resting on pale bleached cement floor tiles. A large mirror behind a stone Buddha image from Indonesia and the soft light give the space an aura of quiet introspection. A large Burmese lacquer work tray sits atop the coffee table in front of the Indonesian day bed.

The long hall, the original *zaal* in the old Dutch house, is now the main living and dining room. A simple teak table and chairs make up the formal dining suite, which is adorned with contemporary Sri Lankan and Balinese paintings. An Indonesian kitchen cabinet glows next to two cane light fittings at the end of the sitting room, on pale bleached cement floor tiles. The black-and-white floor theme is continued in the cushions on a bench at one end of the living area and in the table napkins.

TOP
The courtyard at the back is occupied almost entirely by a swimming pool. The atmosphere of a water garden is highlighted by the sound of water overflowing from the large pots that mark the steps into the pool.

ABOVE
The street entrance to the house is through a simple gate. The latticework trellis, though newly made, was inspired by nineteenth-century houses abutting the street—as was the distressed blue paintwork.

RIGHT
Sharing space with the pool—the main focus of the inner courtyard—the bedroom and service wing and the dining pergola are supported by muted wooden posts, contributing to the atmosphere of tranquility and peace.

a timber pergola, which will eventually be a bower of magenta bougainvillea, is an attractive area for alfresco dining. The courtyard gives the impression of a great water court, with fountains gurgling out of the cement pots that mark the steps into the pool.

On one side of the courtyard is the two-story building that has been built on the site of what must have been the original service wing of this modest house, and on the other the ochre-painted wall of the adjoining property. The new wing houses some of the service areas and the main bedrooms of the house. The addition is clearly modern but respects the proportions and style of the Dutch-period original building with which it shares the site.

The house is furnished with an eclectic mix of simple modern furniture and the occasional piece purchased from other parts of the world, as well as Sri Lankan art. Uncluttered and without fuss, the house is a truly relaxing retreat for the busy owner.

Galle Face Court Apartment

COLOMBO 3 | ARCHITECT: EDWARDS, REID AND BEGG

The Galle Face Court was built in 1934 by the Marckan Marker family in the heart of Colombo, overlooking the green that is the main public space of the city. Built in an age of largesse, the apartments have high ceilings and generously sized rooms—certainly of a size larger than most contemporary houses in Colombo! Most of the apartments boast magnificent views of the city, especially the ones on the upper floors and those facing north, which overlook the gardens of the Taj Samudra Hotel and the Galle Face Green. The building itself was designed and built by Edwards, Reid and Begg, British architects practicing in Sri Lanka, who introduced a liberal blend of Byzantine detailing. A second Galle Face Court was built a little later and is equally elegant and spacious.

The apartment shown here is located on the top floor of the building. In decorating it, the owners opted for an eclectic mix of old and new infused with a decidedly contemporary approach to color inspired by the brilliant hues of Sri Lankan culture. The result is a home that is vibrant and earthy, yet stylish and practical.

Each room is done out in a different color theme, which sets the mood of the space. In the context of the whole, these brilliant colors are used in a clever way. Viewed from one direction, the main rooms are a soothing white. The white-painted exposed roof structure, composed of iron trusses and boarded ceiling, lends height and air to the space and plays a unifying role. In the other direction, viewed from the dining room, the spaces are alive with color, the warm red of the dining room contrasting with the bright ochre in the distant lounge. The polished teak floor, with tinges of both colors, unifies the whole.

RIGHT
The fiery red walls of the dining room are in dramatic contrast to the neutral white of the main sitting room. Beyond, the ochre walls of the anteroom add further fire to the décor. The original 1930s fanlights are echoed in the broad archways separating the almost open-plan space.

LEFT
A modified corner version of a traditional colonial-period couch is piled with cushions in vibrant hand-woven cotton fabrics designed by Barbara Sansoni of Barefoot. The design fabric shop has been an inspiration to many for color and style in contemporary Sri Lanka.

BELOW
Gilt-framed mirrors reflect the brilliantly colored walls in the dining room and anteroom beyond, forming changing works of art. The round table is surrounded by dining chairs after a design by Frank Lloyd Wright, but made from Sri Lankan timber by local craftsmen. The sideboard is 1930s, as is the original fan from the building.

CLOCKWISE FROM TOP LEFT
Vermilion walls surround an original 1930s fanlight. In a corner of the ante-room, green *dracaena* leaves contrast with pink and orange paintwork. Late evening sun paints a wall in several shades of color in the bedroom. A small brass Buddha image in the seventeenth-century Kandyan style sits amid offerings of river stones and orchids on a table in the sitting room.

The entrance to the apartment is up a flight of stairs and along an entrance hall furnished with picture stands supporting paintings of local life by British artist Alex Stewart. The stands and the lighting give the impression of an art gallery. Bright light enters the hallway through a wall of glass blocks installed at one end.

The rest of the furniture is kept to a minimum. In the anteroom to the living room, a simplified and modified copy of a traditional wooden sofa is piled with cushions in brilliant hues. The sitting room is furnished with simple white cotton-covered sofas and the dining room with a solid round wooden table and reproductions of a 1930s Frank Lloyd Wright chair. Gilt-framed mirrors hung above the sideboard reflect the colors of the walls behind, almost as though they were constantly changing contemporary paintings! Strong lines and a rich riot of color make for a décor that is both fun and practical.

The Cinnamon House

GALLE FORT | ARCHITECT: ROHAN JAYAKODY

No. 41, Lighthouse Street was once a large house in the Fort of Galle with the typical plan of veranda, front rooms, hall, back veranda and service rooms along one side of the back courtyard garden. Like many others of its type, various reasons led it to being subdivided by its owners, and the division was made by simply drawing a line on the survey plan of the site and building a wall across. The land was divided with bitter consequences for the beautiful house. One half was left with a miniscule courtyard and all the service buildings while the other was left with a part of the front section and no service areas.

Most people would have demolished the whole building and built a separate and more convenient house on the miniscule 2476 square feet (230 square meters) of land. To the present owner, however, this was a wonderful opportunity to own a pied-à-terre in the Fort at a time when property prices were spiraling. This fact had been overlooked by many prospective buyers, simply because the property was incomplete. But with a little bit of ingenuity and some physical extension, a charmingly eclectic residence has been created from "the half with a part of the front section." The front of the house was renovated and a new and distinctive, albeit small, entrance

created opening out on to Lighthouse Street. The large front room was turned into the entrance hall and the back room converted into a small reception area. Beyond this is sheer fantasy—a unique spatial experience that is anything but a conventional house!

A small courtyard between the existing structure and the extension is thickly planted with bamboo, banana trees and a coconut palm! From this courtyard, a steep staircase leads up to a bedroom and bar above, with the possibility of accessing further terraces and rooftop gardens beyond. At ground level, the stone paving of the courtyard continues uninterrupted through the whole site, inside and outside, to reach the slightly elevated back garden. The nearer section of the covered area is arranged as a sitting area and the section closer to the courtyard as a dining area. A steep flight of antique wooden stairs leads to a bedroom on a mezzanine above the dining area.

This whole house is almost like a bazaar, filled with a fascinating cornucopia of artifacts and memorabilia amassed from a lifetime of avid collecting. Anything and everything that seems to relate together is arranged with no restraint, sometimes bordering on deliberate vulgarity! The resulting experience is the epitome of delightful eclecticism.

LEFT
Dusk brings out the firelight on the rooftop terrace, accessed via a staircase from the back terrace.

RIGHT
A stone bowl embedded in the floor is strewn with fresh flowers as a gesture of welcome in this decidedly medieval entrance hall. A collection of hunting trophies fill the walls above the door and the arch. An exquisite eighteenth century trade cloth with a tree of life motif hangs above a grouping of old Dutch-period boxes. Standing sentinel in a corner of the hall is an *ashva vahanam* or horse chariot discarded from a Hindu temple. The unusual fanlight in the door has been created around a central crystal sphere.

LEFT
Chinese ancestral portraits mirror the Sri Lankan ones on the opposite wall in the lounge area.

ABOVE
Guests are greeted by a collection of trophy heads on the walls above both door and arch. Most are made of wood but with real antlers attached. Here, the almost paired wooden heads display antlers of the spotted deer, which sheds them annually to grow new ones. The buffalo's head is the work of an early taxidermist, as are the two heads of female sambar on either side of it.

RIGHT
The brass candelabra in the lounge area was made by local craftsmen from drawings of the eighteenth-century original. Above the linen-covered sofa, ancestral portraits of important personages in the colonial administration are mixed with nineteenth-century prints of cupids and allegorical scenes of love and retribution, together with a Lionel Wendt photograph of the sunset. The old carpet below the coffee table picks up the red in the ancestral portraits in the otherwise ochre area.

LEFT ABOVE
From the back garden, a steep staircase leads to a terrace outside the main bedroom, also accessible from the bar in the front, and above this a roof terrace offering stunning views over the rooftops of the old fort city of Galle.

LEFT BELOW
Entrance is through an old door with an unusual fanlight incorporating a crystal ball. The writing over the door, *honi soit qui maly pense*, means "shame to who thinks ill of this." Miniature banana palms in ceramic pots flank the door.

BELOW
The dining area overlooks the courtyard garden at the back, bordered by a high wall of laterite blocks. The warm honey-colored glow of the stone harmonizes with the traditional *samara* color of the whole building and the old granite block floor laid throughout the ground floor. The stairs on the side lead up to a second bedroom on a mezzanine above the dining area. The fretwork doors set into the back wall screen an outdoor bathing area. The marble portrait bust atop an eighteenth-century cupboard in the dining area is but one of the numerous fascinating artifacts that add interest to the house.

79, Leyn Baan Street

GALLE FORT | DESIGNER: OLIVIA RICHLEY

The old fort city of Galle has seen a long line and miscellany of residents, some of whom came as invaders and others as traders and investors. Most stayed on for a time and left their mark on the houses and buildings they constructed. The original Portuguese builders of the fort as well as the later Dutch, British and Asian invaders and traders left indelible traces of their tastes and styles in an incredible variety of buildings within the walls of the old fort. Nowhere in Sri Lanka is this built history of the colonial and even the immediate post-colonial periods more clearly visible than here.

The house at No. 79, Leyn Baan Street is a late nineteenth-century British-period restoration on an eighteenth-century Dutch plan, further restored for ease of contemporary living in the early twenty-first century. During the restoration, great care was taken to highlight wherever possible the original splendor of the house's stained-glass doors and antique terracotta tiles. Where this was not always possible, sensitive alternatives have been blended in to make the house both comfortable and convenient.

Following the plan of the classic Dutch town house, the formal entrance is through a veranda at the front of the house. A solid wood-paneled and stained-glass door opens into a hall or *zaal* with two spaces on either side, one used as a formal dining room and the other as a sitting room. Beyond the hall, demarcated by an arched doorway and arched windows, is an in-between space that formed the back veranda to the original building. This opens into a back area now occupied by two buildings. On one side is the original eighteenth-century single-story staff and service wing and on the other a two-story wing added possibly in the late nineteenth century. The upper floor of this wing is now entirely taken up by the owner's bedroom. The two wings flank a very thin courtyard now occupied by a long pond with stone receptacles

RIGHT
The terrace outside the master bedroom is sheltered by a bamboo and timber frame. The cotton-covered bed is the perfect spot for an afternoon siesta cooled by the breezes that blow in from the nearby Indian Ocean.

RIGHT
The upper-floor gallery outside the master bedroom is constructed from fine timber members and overlooks the half-round tiled roofs of the surrounding buildings.

BELOW
A massive teakwood table from Indonesia occupies the dining end of the hall. Indonesian and Sri Lankan textiles form a colorful backdrop to memorabilia on the cement sideboard at the far end.

ABOVE
The hall opens into an in-between space that was formerly the old veranda to the original back garden, now occupied by a building from the nineteenth-century renovation. Sri Lankan stag heads guard the access to the rear courtyard, filled with a long pond with overflowing stone receptacles.

RIGHT
A garage door made from old timber door sashes forms a fascinating entrance from the back street on the ancient rampart.

brimming with water. A later addition of a roof terrace, accessible from the back garden, and the gallery of the upper floor of the bedroom overlook the ancient rampart and modern lighthouse.

The decoration in the interior is suitably eclectic, reflecting the owner's sojourns in other countries and her artistic taste. However, the furniture and effects are arranged and used in such a way as to exude the grace of an old colonial home. The formal sitting area at one end of the main hall is decorated with a mixture of comfortable seats, while a massive rustic teakwood dining table from Indonesia dominates the other end. The white-painted floors in this room, along with glass skylights, compensate for the loss of light brought about by the second building in the courtyard and gives the room the appearance of an outside space in itself. The small but comfortable bedrooms are decorated in a variety of styles with collections gathered over many years of travel.

LEFT
A terrazzo bathtub in one of the guest bedrooms is framed by a highly decorative stained-glass window from the British-period restoration. The terracotta floor tiles are part of the original Dutch house.

RIGHT
The master bed, covered with many layers of exotic cloth and draped with mosquito netting, catches the breezes from the Indian Ocean. The stark white lighthouse and ramparts are visible through the window on the right.

Eden House

GALLE FORT | ARCHITECT: RANJAN ALUVIHARE

Eden House in the Fort of Galle is as flamboyant and full of *joie de vivre* as its owners. The house is a celebration—an eclectic stage set—of travel and experience and sensuality that is only possible in the tropics. Redolent of journeys to the East, it is indeed in the East and at the heart of one of the great entrepôts of trade up to the seventeenth century. It is a fantasy brought to life!

The house, located in the original market square of Galle, is entered through a small courtyard off the street. A simple veranda leads to the dramatic entrance hall, reminiscent of some great Moroccan kasbah. The vaulted ceiling is softly and mysteriously lit from a cornice above. Portraits of long-dead and living relatives line the walls, in the style of an English country house. In the main body of the old house is a kitchen that swerves out into a dining room in one of the wings. This space, too, evokes the mysteries and romance of the Mediterranean through a trompe l'oeil of a stone-lined courtyard complete with a Spanish orange tree! A sitting room occupies the other part of the old house.

It is at the back of the house, however, that the owners have given full rein to their fantasies. Here, the two wings flanking the space are a fantastic evocation of a Moroccan courtyard. Plain plaster columns are brought to life by trellised arches that glow at night from concealed lighting. An ornate wrought-iron balustrade, protruding half-round roof tiles and brick paving laid in a herring-bone pattern add to the flamboyant ambience. An ancient mango tree and a coconut palm add a green twist. Pale flagstone flooring under the colonnades and muted walls make the space appear much bigger than it actually is. The upper level of one wing is a flat-roof terrace on which an industrial chimney camouflages a water tower. The rooms on the upper floor of the other wing are reached by a circular staircase and a long veranda.

The house is filled with a variety of furniture and artifacts gathered from various experiences and existences that the owners have had: China, Morocco, the United Kingdom, India and Indonesia are all represented. Objects and colors are thrown together with gay abandon but come together in an amusing and pleasing way, contributing to a style of decoration that is as eclectic as any to be seen.

BELOW
The Moroccan style of the
courtyard derives from
pointed arches fashioned
from timber latticework.
Lighting adds romantic
glamor to the space.

RIGHT
The flat-roofed terrace above the dining room is an ideal location for entertaining under the stars. The "chimney" near by hides the water tank. On the opposite wing, a balcony with an ornate wrought-iron balustrade leads to the bedrooms.

BELOW
The kitchen area is an integral part of the main living area. Here, the counters are made from solid antique timber. Adding interest is an old window adopted as a spice cupboard, and a set of billiard table lights hanging above the cooking area. Open shelves are filled with kitchenware and a miscellany of items.

CLOCKWISE FROM TOP LEFT
An Indonesian day bed with silk throw cushions in part of the sitting room next to the kitchen. The contemporary paintings are by Sri Lankan artists. The lamp on the ledge is made from an upturned antique betel nut tray dressed in a modern cotton shade. In another part of the sitting room, bric-a-brac and other objects surround an armchair made of water hyacinth stems. Gracing the floor is a tribal rug possibly from Afghanistan via Pakistan. An old door from a Hindu household in the north finds new life at the entrance to the house and is flanked by two magnificent brass roof finials, also from the north. The spiral staircase to the bedroom wing is made from railway sleepers affixed to a concrete column.

RIGHT
A trompe l'oeil of a Mediterranean courtyard forms a highly unusual backdrop in the dining room, which is lit by a skylight from the terrace above. Solid Indonesian benches form the main seating on either side of a long teakwood table adorned with Burmese lacquerware and a vase of colorful flowers. A handsome nineteenth-century ebony and jackwood linen cupboard stands against the wall. The strong lines of the furniture are softened with blue swabs and blue-and-white cushions.

Helga's Folly

KANDY | ARCHITECT: MINETTE DE SILVA

The hills surrounding the medieval capital of Kandy are now dotted with residences that take advantage of the spectacular view overlooking the lake and the ancient Temple of the Tooth. Nestled in lush vegetation at the eastern end of the lake, and set well above it, is what for a long time was known as the Chalet Hotel. Now called Helga's Folly, the modernist guest house, originally designed by the owner's aunt, Minette de Silva, in the 1960s, has been transformed into a lush manifestation of an extraordinarily flamboyant and creative lifestyle. From top to bottom, the guest house is a reflection of the theatrical tastes and eclectic style of Helga, its owner.

Clues as to what awaits the visitor are apparent in the slightly overgrown road and pathway to the guest house and the even more overgrown entranceway and car park. The front entrance, almost hidden among a profusion of bougainvillea and tumbergia, opens to a hall from whence begins a veritable Aladdin's cave of visual delight.

The hall inside the doorway, in what might once have been a small, uninspiring room, now has the authority of a great hall. Large candlesticks, overladen with years of dripping wax, offer welcome. Dark walls create a sense of cave-like mystery. Above all, no space or surface is left untouched. Inspired by the rich textures and colors of the Kandyan landscape, every nook is a new discovery that delights the senses, and every step must be taken carefully lest one loses oneself in the myriad objects and the experiences they recall. Exquisite antiques vie for attention with basketfuls of plastic flowers. Modernist paintings from the 43rd Group hang on walls papered with pages from the gossip columns.

The adjoining salon on the ground floor opens out to a lushly planted garden through large French windows. Here, Art Deco carpets and early 1930s furniture are juxtaposed with

RIGHT
Upstairs, the red dining room at the far end is reached through a whimsical ceremonial arch of shy cherubs. In the blue dining room in the foreground, family photos are hung over an allegorical landscape. Teak flooring unites the two spaces.

RIGHT
The salon opens to the garden through fiery red doors. The nineteenth-century cupboard, the classic Galle *almirah*, here with decorative ebony trimmings and embellishments, stands in marked contrast to the simple teak 1950s living room set adorned with brilliantly hued silk cushions. On the walls, a fine collection of Kandyan spears vies with an assortment of paintings, puppets, pots and other items, including timber deer heads with genuine antlers, a long tradition in rural Sri Lanka.

BELOW
Dressed to kill, the staff stand to attention behind a table in the red dining room. The wall behind is painted with a blow-up of a traditional painting of a king in procession. The red background is typical of seventeenth- and eighteenth-century schools of painting in Sri Lanka.

RIGHT
The front of the guest house is painted a dark green to harmonize with the surrounding foliage. Lively red-painted sculptures on the balcony and the red French doors from the salon pick up the colors in the garden shrubs.

BELOW
Inspired by the frescoes of Sigiriya, Cloud Maidens float on the stairway walls amidst celestial foliage.

ornately carved late Dutch-period cupboards. Walls are hung with a profusion of graphic art, collections of stag horns and antique spears. The predominant colors of ochre and red team up with the dark furniture to create a warm and comfortable ambience.

Red in one area and blue in another characterize the upper-floor dining rooms. A varied collection of chairs and tables are set to different themes of color and detail. In the red area, a blown-up version of a painting from a Kandyan temple forms the backdrop at the buffet, while a soft blue theme creates a moody atmosphere in the dining room.

Each bedroom has been stamped with its own individuality on the whim and fancy of the owner, the objects used and the quality of light and views available. The interconnecting spaces and bathrooms go their own way with one bathroom painted as an aquarium and another entirely plastered with pages from magazines of yesteryear. The whole house brims with an enjoyment of every aspect of life, where each object is valued not for its monetary cost, but by the sheer pleasure it gives the owner and her guests.

LEFT
Magazine covers, post-cards and love letters form an intense collage in the guest toilet with its built-in water closet and tall nineteenth-century cistern.

RIGHT
A set of ceiling panels painted in the old Kandyan style is a striking backdrop to a seating area in the blue bedroom, furnished with 1930s-style chairs and side tables and a 1960s coffee table.

BELOW LEFT
Hand-painted butterflies flit in the light of the glass door to the garden in the red bedroom.

BELOW RIGHT
Copious silverware and white table settings give the blue dining room an ethereal look.

Contemporary Interpretations

In 1948 Sri Lanka regained independence after 450 years of colonial rule. This event proved to be a major catalyst for a resurgence in Sri Lankan art, literature and architecture.

The first public buildings to be associated with newly independent Sri Lanka appealed to nationalist sentiments. The University of Peradeniya near Kandy by Shirley de Alwis, and the Independence Memorial Hall in Colombo by Neville Wynne-Jones, appropriated ancient Sri Lankan styles and motifs. Although these buildings seemed to represent a retreat into pastiche, they nevertheless succeeded in inspiring a new generation of architects to re-examine Sri Lankan traditions.

The modern Sri Lankan house developed out of a fusion of Sri Lankan vernacular traditions and European modernist ideals. European modernism took a tenuous hold in the Colombo of the 1930s though Art Deco, and "modern" took precedence over pure modernism. A milestone building, which appeared during the war years of 1939–45, was the block of flats in the Colombo Fort designed for Baur and Company by Goldman and Maillart. It was Andrew Boyd, however, who designed the first truly modern buildings in Sri Lanka, with a house in Kandy in 1939 and another couple of houses in Colombo in 1946.

Minette de Silva was not only one of the first truly modern Sri Lankan architects, but was also probably the first formally qualified Asian woman architect. After training in Bombay and the Architectural Association (AA) School of Architecture in the UK, she became associated with Le Corbusier through meetings of the CIAM (Congres Internationaux d'Architecture Moderne) group during the 1940s and early 1950s. Back in her home country, she was determined to follow Le Corbusier's advice of drawing on her own traditions for inspiration. In a series of houses built in the 1950s, Minette established a style of modern, open-plan building with many of the living spaces flowing into the landscape. Wherever possible and appropriate, she used the work of local artisans.

At the time of independence, the architectural profession was still in its infancy. One by one, the expatriate practices which had flourished before the war closed their doors, and a new generation of Sri Lankans left to study architecture abroad. One of the most significant of these was Valentine Gunasekera. Trained at the AA, Gunasekera had worked with Eero Saarinen in the United States. In his work in Sri Lanka, he attempted to adapt modern abstract formalism to the tropical

PREVIOUS PAGE
The stark all-white concrete and glass Havelock Town House (page 126), with its design illusions to Mies van der Rohe, Le Corbusier and Richard Meier, is an example of a design direction gaining ground in the suburbs of Colombo.

ABOVE
Simple upholstered chairs arrayed around a glass-topped teak table harmonize with the hues and materials of the rest of the Havelock Town House. Tall sliding glass doors open on to a narrow area at the back of the site planted with towering areca nut palms.

context. The most striking of his buildings is the highly original Tangalla Bay Hotel of 1974.

Also returning to the island after training at the AA was Geoffrey Bawa, who in 1957 took over the then moribund British practice of Edwards, Reid and Begg. Working with his associate Ulrik Plesner, he also experimented with various alternatives to the prevalent styles. After an early flirtation with "tropical modernism," Bawa discovered the virtues of vernacular building traditions. His most seminal work, the Ena de Silva House of 1960, is a fusion of these modernist planning ideals. This, in turn, led to his masterly design for the Bentota Beach Hotel of 1968, which fused the traditions of a Sinhalese *walauwe* manor with the modernist plan of Le Corbusier.

Influential also was artist and designer Ena de Silva. Her work in batik, and her collaborations with her son Anil Gamini Jayasooriya and Laki Senanayake, the artist who started work as an assistant in Bawa's office, produced artifacts that were used extensively in the work of the architects at the time and summed up the new Sri Lankan spirit. An eclectic series of inspirations, including patterns and idioms derived from ancient and medieval Sri Lankan flags and banners, led to commissions ranging from table linen to

the 50-foot (15-meter) banners that adorned the lobby of the Colombo Oberoi designed by Skidmore, Owings and Merrill in 1974. The most striking of her works, however, was a ceiling designed for the Bentota Beach Hotel. De Silva now runs a cooperative in her native village dedicated to a revival of local arts and crafts. Products from this and other efforts towards the rejuvenation of traditional crafts are very much a part of the contemporary Sri Lankan interior design scene.

The resurgence in traditional crafts with a modern design twist is evident in the handlooms produced by Barefoot, the design and cloth shop at 704 Galle Road, Colombo, which is a labyrinthine collector's dream. Barbara Sansoni, with her incredible eye for color, has done for Sri Lankan handloom cotton what Jim Thomson did for Thai silk. Stunning designs and vibrant colors are the hallmark of Sansoni's work, which she continues with a dedicated band of designers and weavers working in rural Sri Lanka. The sarong, the quintessential garment of Asian men (and women) has been transformed forever into a particularly colorful Sri Lankan version by Barefoot and is now copied by many other designers, including the mass producers for the Sri Lankan market in India.

ABOVE
A Rolls Royce coupé from the 1930s forms an unusual "sculpture" in the entrance-cum-garage to the House on 33rd Lane. An eighteenth-century ebony wood sofa is paired with a steel chair designed for the Kandalama Hotel. Next to the painting by Belgian artist Saskia Pringiers is the entrance to the studio office and the guest rooms and roof terrace on the upper level.

Other products from the Barefoot range, and from other designers inspired by it, make up a major component of contemporary interiors. Objects of everyday use, such as table napkins and bedspreads, curtains and cushion covers, tablecloths and towels use vibrant cotton handlooms. These handloom products, in brilliant hues and stunning designs, have come to infiltrate even the most conservative of Sri Lankan homes, making them an essential part of the contemporary design ethos.

This has also led to a revival of the local handloom industry. Under the guidance of Chandra Thenuwara of the National Craft Council, the local handloom centers in the provinces began to produce material that took into consideration the demands of the local market. Today, many of these centers produce contemporary designs that have a distinctly Sri Lankan feel to them. These explorations were further reinforced by government policies of self-reliance promoted by the left-of-center politics of the immediate post-colonial period. Imports were restricted, as was travel abroad. This did not mean, however, that there was a dearth of ideas or inspiration from the goings on in other parts of the world. Indeed, the early 1960s restriction of goods and travel abroad brought about a creative blossoming in the architecture and design of the island. Access to foreign magazines as well as communication with foreign visitors to the country also inspired local designers, as did the various expatriates who came out to Sri Lanka to live and work.

All these changes prompted designers to re-examinine and work with local resources. The handloom cloth industries, along with many local building material industries and crafts people, were employed to good effect. By the 1970s a Sri Lankan ethos of using available skills and materials to best possible advantage was part of the Sri Lankan architectural and design consciousness. Good Sri Lankan design was also seen to be moving towards buildings and spaces that were open to the natural environment, and utilized as many local resources as possible. Terracotta tiles for both floors and roofs, plain polished cement for floors, rush and coconut coir carpets, coconut timber columns, rafters and structural members, handloom and locally manufactured batik fabrics teamed naturally with landscapes full of frangipani to form a unique Sri Lankan contemporary style.

Since the introduction of a market economy in 1977, new materials and technologies have been introduced to Sri Lanka, adding to the historically strong colonial influences.

More frequent and continuous relations with foreign countries and travel abroad by an increasing number of Sri Lankans for study and business have made Sri Lankan design sensitive to global ideas. Changes have also occurred as new technologies and materials are being teamed with more cheaply and easily available local ones. An example of this is the collaboration of Swiss furniture designer Rico Tarawella and Bentota craftsmen of the Workshop, whose furniture combines modern welding techniques with traditional materials such as timber and leather.

In the world of architecture, the work of Chelvadurai Anjalendran and Vijitha Basnayake stands out. Light, eco-conscious buildings and the use of sustainable and easily available materials are very much a part of contemporary residential architecture. Living rooms open out to gardens and courtyards. Bathrooms are open-air. Sensitivity to the environment and to budgetary considerations is also evident in the widespread use of recycled building materials, not only antique doors, windows or columns, but more modern and recent materials such as railway sleepers and steel girders, timber rafters and old floors, cement and ceramic tiles and even metal or terracotta roofing. Overall, good Sri Lankan design seems to have developed an eye for sensible, practical materials as much as for economy of use.

Increasing congestion in Colombo and rising house prices have also impacted on the design of the contemporary Sri Lankan house. With most suburban houses being built on less than 3000 square feet (280 square meters) of land in increasingly congested suburbs, the internal courtyard, the garden and innovations to the way light and ventilation are provided to the interior have become important design considerations.

Worldwide design trends are also influencing interior design schemes. A major influence on the contemporary Sri Lankan interior is the work of designer and entrepreneur Shanth Fernando of Paradise Road, who is credited with giving Sri Lanka a "style identity," making local arts and crafts very chic but, at the same time, "timeless." Fernando uses local skills to manufacture a variety of home decoration items that are inspired by local traditional craft but, under his direction, with an eye on international design trends. The gallery and restaurant opened by him in the old offices of Edwards, Reid and Begg have set new trends in the dining experience and found a new life for a significant contemporary building.

RIGHT
This bathroom in the Havelock Town House (page 126) is a tactile and visual delight. Clean lines, a muted palette and natural materials inject a Zen air. Separated by a frosted glass partition, a solid plank of teak floats over a chest of drawers to form a vanity stand, while timber "carpets" are laid over a mosaic tile floor. Lighting is subtle, hidden away in the ceiling and in alcoves on the wall.

LEFT
A weathered old bench
sits below the deep over-
hanging eaves of the
loggia. The polished satinwood (*Cloroxylon sweita-
nia*) columns, raised on
elegant granite bases,
are from a time when this
timber was an abundant
building material.

RIGHT
The forecourt at the front
of the house is floored
with river stones and a
massive millstone. A roof
of half-round tiles on a
timber frame shelters the
path to the magnificent
antique temple door, the
main entrance to the house.

Alfred Place House

COLOMBO 3 | ARCHITECT: GEOFFREY BAWA

No. 5, Alfred Place, built in 1963, more than
any other building of this period contains the
thinking of the architect Geoffrey Bawa that
came to epitomize his work. Inspired by the
demands of the owner, artist and designer
Ena de Silva, who came from a family steeped
in tradition, for a house that would incorpo-
rate traditional Sri Lankan elements—an en-
closing wall, open-sided rooms, verandas and
courtyards—as well as modern elements such
as an office, studio and guest wing, Bawa
responded instinctively to the challenge of
the small urban site. For the first time in Sri
Lankan contemporary architectural history,

the open planning tradition of the modern
movement is blended harmoniously with traditional Sri Lankan elements and materials
and techniques of construction to form a
seamless whole: the inward-looking family
rooms and service areas, work spaces and
guest rooms are all clearly defined and separated but at the same time interconnected.

The main spaces of the house are arranged in layers of increasing privacy as they
move inwards away from the street. Behind
an austere plaster wall punctuated only by
a solid wooden door and the entrance to the
garage, a river stone-paved forecourt forms

RIGHT
The study, immediately to the left of the entrance, looks over the main internal courtyard. Like all the rooms in the house, this one is naturally ventilated from two sides. Louvered shutters replace glass windows. A projecting bay window wraps around to form a desk and a setting for a nineteenth-century terracotta roof finial. A painting by the occupant, artist Saskia Pringiers, hangs above the desk.

BELOW
A single plank of *para para* (*Samanea saman*) makes a magnificent dining table on the loggia. A mixture of nineteenth-century office chairs and an eighteenth-century Wolfendhal chair form the seating. Enamel-coated studio lamps light up the table at night. The artist's works, stacked up against the wall, blend into the setting of stone, weathered timber, white plaster and terracotta tiles.

a buffer between the street and a magnificent old door, rescued from a temple, which opens to a narrow passage leading to the large central courtyard surrounded on all four sides by a low-eaved colonnade of satinwood and presided over by an ancient frangipani (*Plumeria rubra*) and a shady mango.

Now occupied by the Belgian artist Saskia Pringiers and her family, the rooms closest to the road house the office, studio, garage and guest suite. At the far end of the courtyard is the main living area—a two-story building with living and dining areas on the ground floor opening on to the courtyard, separated by a timber-lined spiral staircase leading to the shrine room and family bedrooms above. Running down one side of the compound is the service area. The whole area is paved with varying textures of stone, from washed river stone in the courtyard to dressed granite in the main spaces. Large millstones define the corners of the courtyard and act as casual seating or for drying things on. Weathered timber, white plaster walls and half-round terracotta tiles are complemented by collections of ancient objects in natural tones.

be free
be free-free
free from attachment
worldly bliss
should you
desire to reach
the freedom of
the skies!!

The seamless transition between inside and out is one of the joys of the house. Built during a time of shortage of modern materials and of import restrictions, the architect made innovative use of the available locally produced materials. The dominant tiled roof and the localized palette of materials gives the house its vernacular feel.

The living room is arranged very much like one of Saskia's paintings. The original built-in seats and niches are filled with objects—a Buddha statue, a traditional drill, textile printing blocks, a food stand, a granite rat—that often reappear in her paintings. The writings on the wall are inspirations and quotations, including one from a dear friend which says "be free, be free, be free from attachment, ... should you desire to reach the freedom of the skies."

Havelock Town House

COLOMBO 5 | ARCHITECT: RAJI KADIRGAMAR

This imposing concrete-and-glass structure, built in the inner suburbs of Colombo, is a decidedly contemporary statement of urban life in the tropics. The neo-modernist look of the house is inspired by the works of the modernists of the early and mid-twentieth century, such as Le Corbusier and Richard Neutra, as well as the great architects of the day, like Richard Meier. The minimal palette of materials—white plaster walls, timber or polished concrete floors and frameless glass fenestrations—creates a calm and tranquil atmosphere, but also enables the house to function as a superb gallery for the owner's collection of contemporary art.

Three modules—a smaller central mass flanked by two larger masses—are arranged in a U shape around an impeccably maintained garden filled with mature frangipani trees, areca palms and other tropical foliage. Frameless glass picture windows bordering a simple and planar terrace lined with a procession of columns create a seamless extension of the inner spaces to the outside.

The entrance to the house is via a long passage parallel to and open on one side to the garden on the right. A collection of line drawings hangs over a simple console table of *para mara* (*Samanea saman*) timber. At the end of the corridor, a slight change of level, indicated by four steps, marks the transition from the entrance to the main entertainment area. Here, the dining room and anteroom-cum-gallery end in the magnificent double-height living room with its bridgeway gallery. Skylights define the circulation from the otherwise open rooms.

Running along the back of these spaces is a linear water court in which is reflected a regularly planted row of areca palms. The high walls of this courtyard allow a soft glow of skylight and occasional rays of sunlight to penetrate down, while the bright tropical light from the garden comes in on the other side.

The dining room is sparsely furnished with minimal contemporary furniture, all set on a pale timber floor and white carpet. Movable wood-framed glass panels become part of the walls, allowing the room to be closed off for intimate dinner parties. The small anteroom between the dining and living rooms is a gallery for a collection of black-and-white sketches. Two simple timber

RIGHT
A single areca palm framed between the columns of the double-height living room emphasizes the verticality of the space. A matching row of palms borders the wall at the back of the site, their tops peeping over the open-air deck. Early afternoon light softens the sculptural but neutral geometry of the architecture.

LEFT
The bridge linking the terrace and the master bedroom overlooks the main living space, which is austerely furnished with teakwood and leather furniture. The paintings and cement sculpture of the Buddha in the background are contemporary Sri Lankan.

ABOVE
Shafts of sunlight paint a picture of light and shadow on the plain wall of the water and areca court. The trunks of areca palms silhouetted against the back wall are living "art."

RIGHT
An *ashva vahanam* from an old temple chariot stands in the doorway of the anteroom, marking a transition from indoors to outdoors.

benches and a coffee table furnish this space. This leads into the main living room with its magnificent double-height volume. Carefully modulated windows reduce the glare of direct sunlight, but manage to flood it with a soft glow of skylight. Here, minimalist contemporary furniture made from rich tropical hardwood is placed on a white carpet on teak floors. More black-and-white sketch studies of the human form by a Dutch artist working in Sri Lanka animate this space. Clear frameless glass picture windows bring the lush tropical outdoors in.

A sky-lit staircase leads to the upper floors. Bedrooms occupy the first level as well as a family room that opens on to an open-air terrace over the dining room and anteroom. A doorway on the terrace leads to the wooden bridgeway over the living room. Above the bedrooms, a roof deck—a stunning glass pavilion—shelters the staircase and allows for contemplation of the rooftops of this leafy suburb of Colombo and the tropical sky.

LEFT
Glass skylights mark the
edge of the dining room
space which, like most
others in this house, flows
from one to another to
the outside. A painting by
Jagath Ravindra anchors
the vista through these
spaces from living room
to entrance corridor.

TOP
On the smoked glass dining
table, two wooden lion
figures from an old temple
chariot pay homage to
a bunch of Arum lilies in
a Spanish glass vase.

ABOVE
One side of the main
entrance passage is open
to the garden. A collection
of line drawings by a
Pakistani artist hangs over
the streamlined console.

House on 33rd Lane

COLOMBO 3 | ARCHITECT: GEOFFREY BAWA

Shortly after Geoffrey Bawa had rented the third of four small houses on a narrow cul-de-sac off 33rd Lane, in 1959, he offered to buy all four from his landlord as and when they fell vacant. No. 4 was the first house to be bought, in 1961, and was added to the original sitting room and bedroom to create a new gallery, dining room and garage. In 1968 the other two houses were acquired and major remodeling undertaken. The actual forms of the original houses are now almost impossible to discern. In their place is an introspective labyrinth of rooms and garden courts that give the impression of infinite and endless space.

From the street, the house appears as a simple façade, its only fenestrations being a large timber-trellised garage door, a similar side door and the main entrance, an acrylic door with an etching of the Sun God that opens into the house. Through this door, in the cool, subdued light, two magnificent cars—a 1935 Rolls Royce and a 1953 Mercedes—are parked on chocks. Past these, a long white corridor leads to the interior of the house past a series of small garden courts, where, turning at 90 degrees past three antique columns, a veranda and further garden court are seen. This is the heart of the house where the architect held court. This is furnished with a long modern sofa covered in handloom fabric, paired with a butterfly chair and a cane armchair. A small round table and an eighteenth-century Indo-Portuguese chair act as a dining and work table. The main bedroom opens off this space, as does the formal sitting room and dining room. When the doors are open in the bedroom, a long vista connects the bed to a frangipani tree outside the formal living room. The dining room, with its epoxy-coated table and classic modern tulip chairs, in turn opens into the back garden court.

At the front of the house, above the garage, is a two-story tower. A winding staircase, starting almost in the garage, leads up to a sitting room and guest bedroom and

further on up to a roof terrace. The sitting room, which also doubles as a library, is lined on one side with hand-painted Balinese cloths and is furnished with a mixture of modern and antique chairs and tables, some designed by Bawa himself. A collection of line drawings of old buildings by Barbara Sansoni hangs on one wall, whilst a beautiful piece of ancient limestone sculpture sits atop an eighteenth-century jackwood cupboard inlaid in ebony and ivory. The partly covered roof garden is filled with plants in built-in troughs and a green travertine table on steel legs. Here, as the sun sets over the horizon to the east, the candle flames provide light for a quiet drink looking out over the suburbs of Colombo.

LEFT
At the end of the long white entrance corridor is a set of doors decorated by Australian artist Donald Friend. Each panel is a view into an idyllic tropical garden from the different levels of a multi-storied pavilion. A terracotta horse and old Chettinad columns define a pool court that is also a pause on the journey from the entrance to the main house veranda. Dalmatians have been constant companions in the house, and posing here is Leopold III.

ABOVE RIGHT
The most frequently used area in the house is the main sitting veranda. On the modern sofa, a combination of woven fabric from Barefoot and batik from the Paradise Road store is combined with gray Jim Thomson silk cushions. Satiric cartoons (not shown) of Colombo society personalities by Geoffrey Bawa's brother Bevis hang above a batik-topped coffee table by Ena de Silva. Balinese wooden birds share the central marble-topped coffee table with a *puffichichie* pan, a brass oil lamp and tailor's scissors. The small sculpture on the rectangular side table is by Indian artist Nandagopal.

FAR LEFT
A table lamp in the second guest room, its base made from a magnetic toy, was designed for the Blue Water Hotel. The bentwood chair is an original Thonet.

LEFT
A wrought-iron candelabra turned bedside lamp lights up the guest bedroom, casting shadows on the nineteenth-century timber and paper alterpiece on the wall. The bed is covered with a Ritan Mazunda de-signed bedspread from Fab India.

The upper-floor sitting
room is an essay in the
architect's style and taste.
Each object—ranging from
third-century Indian sculpture to modern toys from
the Museum of Modern
Art in New York—is chosen
for its intrinsic beauty or
amusement and arranged
to blend harmoniously
together. The wall on the
left is covered in a magnificent collection of Balinese
cloths made during the
architect's journeys to Bali
whilst building a house
for the artist Donald Friend.
The sofa is to the archi-
tect's own design whilst
the bentwood chair is
an original Thonet. The
easy chairs are a design
adopted for the Bentota
Beach Hotel, built in 1969.

Hameed House

KOTTE | ARCHITECT: C. ANJALENDRAN

Located on a sloping site on one of the many hills that comprise the Colombo suburb of Nawala, the Hameed House effectively combines modern and recycled elements and a clever use of site and space to achieve a private yet truly tropical living experience. The house has been sensitively imposed on the landscape, the sloping site and its situation being used to maximum advantage. A steep rise to the east was built up to allow for views over the surrounding treetops and rooftops. On fine days during the northeast monsoon, the silhouette of Adams Peak is visible in the far distance.

Reached down a steep driveway, the house presents an austere and strict façade, broken only by a set of beautiful antique doors salvaged by the owner from his family mosque, a victim of the often mindless modernization that affects many old public buildings in Sri Lanka. The simple brief given to the architect, C. Anjalendran, was to fit the immense doors into the design, a pleasurable task given the architect's fascination, in his own words, with "the continuity and the context of the traditional in relation to modern lifestyles and aspirations." The doors lead into the garage and the interior garden beyond.

Internally, the house is conceived as two large, pavilion-like verandas, one on top of the other, to which are attached a row of rooms. A formal sitting room at a half level connects the two verandas. The ground-floor veranda, entered through the garage from the driveway, is a casual sitting area and dining room, which opens out directly into the garden. A guest suite occupies one end of this veranda and a staircase leads off the other to the formal sitting room on the half-landing level of the stairs, which is formally furnished with an eclectic mix of contemporary and antique furniture, including an eighteenth-century Dutch chest. Glazed doors open out to a garden terrace on the same level.

The staircase continues up to reach the upper-level veranda, which comprises the family living room. A double colonnade of concrete and antique timber columns provides extra shade from the sun and rain, and plant troughs bring the garden into the space. Like the veranda below, this is totally open to the elements with no glazing or windows. Off this veranda, magnificent high antique doors open into the bedrooms.

BELOW
An Indian printed cloth by
Ritan Mazunda of Fab India
is the centerpiece of the
middle-level formal sitting
room. Comfortable modern
sofas interspersed with

nineteenth-century easy
chairs, a charming Dutch-
period chest and other
collectibles harmonize
with the clean lines of the
architecture that make this
space one with the outside.

ABOVE
The entrance veranda,
paved in traditional terracotta tiles, ends in the
dining room at the far end,
with the stairs to the next
level rising behind it.
Abundant vegetation and
the small pool in the middle
distance make the area
feel like an extension of
the garden rather than an
internal part of the house.

LEFT
A nineteenth-century cup-
board with porcelain knobs
is the focus of the dining
area. The stainless steel
and leather chairs are an
interpretation of a chair
originally made in metal
and rattan in the office of
architect Geoffrey Bawa.

RIGHT
The two verandas are con-
nected by a formal sitting
room reached by a brass-
railed staircase. The clean
sweep of the roof gives
the whole space a sense
of generous spaciousness.

Weeraman Walauwe

WELIGAMA | DESIGNER: SASKIA PRINGIERS

Weeraman Walauwe in Weligama is the country home of Belgian artist Saskia Pringiers and her husband, who have long made Sri Lanka their second home. The house itself is in the style of the early to mid-twentieth century bungalows built by the prosperous landowning and entrepreneurial class of Sri Lanka. Set on a commanding site overlooking vast tracts of paddy fields that may have once belonged to the family, the house is essentially composed of two parts. The early and more formal part is the classic porch leading to a veranda flanked by two front rooms. A long hallway is divided into a living and formal dining space by a decorative arch and this, in turn, opens out to a back veranda. Two other rooms open off the dining area. In later years, a service wing appears to have been added, reached via the back veranda.

The most recent renovations have involved additions and alterations to the back of the house where a new service wing and formal dining room have been added, creating a private courtyard. The biggest change to the house, however, has been in the way it is lived in by the artist and her family.

Entry to the compound is through a side entrance along a lane off the main road. The entry court is complete with garages, a boat shed and staff quarters and is casually planted with plants typical of a village garden. A path across the lawn leads to the front of the house with its view over the surrounding paddy fields. A swimming pool with an infinity edge, surrounded by a paved deck and grass, sits beneath a large and spreading mango tree. The porch of the old house denotes the entrance and is now used as an extension of

RIGHT
The dining room is an extension of the back veranda. Here, polished cement floors and dining table are teamed with reproductions of eighteenth-century Wolfendhal chairs. The folded concrete staircase leads to the guest rooms in the attic. A collection of antique pottery sits atop an eighteenth-century jackwood dowry chest.

ABOVE
Stones weigh down the
branches of a fragrant
frangipani in the rear courtyard overlooked by a pair
of nineteenth-century nurs-
ing chairs and an upturned
mortar which serves as a
coffee table. The copper
cauldron may once have
boiled rice in the kitchens
of this old manor house.

RIGHT
The classic and elegant
front of the house is typical
of those built in the early
twentieth century by the
local élite.

the veranda. The whole central space acts as
a sitting room with a suite of bedrooms on
either side. This space leads into the extensive
back veranda that now connects the dining
room and service area to the right and the
artist's studio on the left. A broad-eaved
colonnaded court with a frangipani in the
center is the focus of this area.

Additional guests are accommodated
in a converted attic accessed via an elegant,
accordian-like cement staircase affixed to one
side of the dining space, which has a matching cement table. The artist's studio occupies
an airy, almost double-height space which
may have been a former service area. Here,
the artist produces her sublime works. The
style of the house is a unique statement of
her inspiration, which is always drawn from
the milieu in which she lives. The dark, earthy
or black-and-white tones of her paintings are
clearly reflected in her taste of interior décor,
which is invariably a display of many of the
objects that inspire her work.

CLOCKWISE FROM TOP LEFT
A Hanukkah is placed on an old Ayurvedic medicine chest with a favorite quotation scribbled on the wall behind. A collection of antique pots sits on top of an eighteenth-century jackwood dowry chest under the polished cement stairs leading to the guest areas. A plaster cast of the *nawa nari khunjare* or the nine woman elephant knot decorates a wall beside the door leading to the kitchen. A detail of a painting in the style of the southern school depicting the Buddha and his disciples.

BELOW
The sitting room, with its original decorative arch and fretwork doors, is an elegant setting for a mix of modern furniture and ancient artifacts. A comfy sofa and chaise longue face an old granite bench which serves as an unusual coffee table. The painting by the resident artist, Saskia Pringiers, was part of a series about identity.

Anjalendran's House

KOTTE | ARCHITECT: C. ANJALENDRAN

The house belongs to an architect who came to the profession via dancing and origami. This perhaps provides the key to understanding his architectural works. Best known for the passion and color he brought to his works for the SOS children's villages, he lives by a simple dictum of not doing for others any architecture which he would not do for himself, or afford to live in. This is epitomized by the small house that he calls his own in the Colombo suburb of Battaramulla.

A colorful door sheltered by a frangipani leads into a garage, which doubles as an office during the week, in which is parked a Bajaj three-wheeler. A passage off the garage leads into the heart of the architect's world. A huge roof soars to an upper sleeping deck, while a small veranda wraps round a courtyard, forming a loggia, with a bedroom on the far side. On warm, sultry nights, an orange jasmine (*Murraya paniculata*) fills the courtyard with fragrance from its delicate white blossoms.

These seemingly simple spaces are the repository of an extraordinary collection of artifacts. The furniture is simple enough, but is of interest in its own right: British-period office chairs blend with Dutch-period cupboards and contemporary steel furniture. The focus of the sitting room is a built-in sofa behind which hangs a diverse collection of paintings with pride of place given to an unusual pink painting by the artist Saskia Pringiers, whose usual earth-colored tones seems to have bowed out in deference to the architect's spirit! The dining room occupies the opposite end of the main space. A row of built-in cupboards acts as a platform for a collection of bronze images of Nataraj dancing before a screen print of flames by local artist Laki Senanayake.

The sanctum sanctorum of the house is the bedroom upstairs. Approached by a steep flight of steps and through an antechamber filled with Buddhist icons, the inner sleeping area is filled with Hindu iconography. The far wall is covered with icons of Lord Krishna from the pilgrimage town of Natwara in India. A miniature Alexander Calder mobile gently rotates above the classic image of Nataraj. A ledge behind the bed itself is filled with at least a hundred different images of Lord Ganesh, the elephant-headed God of Wisdom. A large batik hanging by Ena de Silva of a bird in flight, taken from an ancient Vedic symbol for creation, hangs behind the images.

The architect once described his house as a tent, and a tent it is when in fading light, with the art softly lit, one sits down to listen to one of his unending collection of ragas, and the house itself seems to disappear under the vast overhanging shelter of the roof.

LEFT
The built-in seat and platform at one end of the main living space are enlivened by an eclectic mix of art and artifacts and colordul cushions. The central painting by Saskia Pringiers is flanked by works by Richard Gabriel and Ivan Peiris, both members of the 43rd Group, and by Laki Senanayake. The Dutch planter's chair, from which the architect usually presides over his guests, is a satinwood copy of a nineteenth-century original. The table is solid *para mara* (*Samanea Saman*) timber. The sculpture of the flying bull on the table is by Tissa Ranasinghe.

A single flight of plain polished cement steps leads
to the upper-floor bedroom-
cum-gallery. At the end of
the dining room, a screen
print by Laki Senanayake
forms a fiery backdrop
to the dancing figures of
Nataraj in front.

FAR LEFT
The dining table does double duty as the architect's
work table. More paintings
adorn the walls.

LEFT
A collection of objects at
the top of the stairs, lit by
sunlight streaming through
an arched window.

Retreats and Resorts

"Tis said that the waters from the fountains of Paradise could be heard from here as it was only 40 leagues to Paradise from here"

—Friar Magnolli, papal emissary to the court of Kublai Khan

Paradise being so close, for centuries Sri Lanka has been thought of as the next best thing. When Adam was expelled from Paradise, it is said that he was given the island as compensation and his first step, according to one legend, was on the top of Adam's Peak, the holy mountain to which adherents of all of Sri Lanka's major religions flock annually.

The oldest retreats in predominantly Buddhist Sri Lanka are, in reality, the ancient monastic complexes. A classic example is the second-century cave complex on the lower slopes of Ritigala mountain, 25 miles (40 km) southwest of the ancient city of Anuradhapura. Here, the ruins still exude an air of a peace and tranquility that revives the soul.

PREVIOUS PAGE
The main sitting room and dining room sit on the edge of the garden defined by the saffron wall and the azure pool. The 70 by 30 foot (21 by 9 meter) pool, which is finished in dark green polished cement, is large enough for users to do laps. The hill side of the pool has an infinity edge that runs off into views of the jungle and Lake Koggala. At the deep end (not shown), a cascade falls from a carved opening.

Built by an Anuradhapura king, the stone pathways that wind through giant trees at the base of Ritigala still call upon one to meditate. Its companion, the forest monastery Arankele, has a monumental pathway that forms the base of this beautiful ruin. With their pavilions and bathhouses, cave dwellings and large refectories, the meditation retreats of old are said to have housed hundreds, if not thousands, who wished to retreat from the trials of everyday life into one of meditation and self-realization. Ruins of these monastic complexes reveal that they were more than simple cells and pathways and meditation halls. Rather, they were devoted to various aspects of meditation and self-realization through rituals of mental and physical cleansing of the mind and body. Bathing houses arranged around central courtyards with pools of hot and cold water, and the paraphernalia needed to prepare ingredients to treat the body, seem suspiciously like modern-day spas. The architecture, however, is characterized by an extreme simplicity of detail and an almost modernist honesty to structure and material. No carving or embellishment mars the beauty of a slab of granite, which is expertly crafted to fulfil its particular role in the whole ensemble.

BELOW
Located at Dambulla, 150 miles (170 km) from Colombo, Kandamala Hotel, built on elongated stilts, occupies a unique site amidst rocky outcrops, lakes and virgin forest.

Such retreats still play an important role in Sri Lanka. People often take time out to retreat into a well-disciplined and structured life around a spiritual theme. Modern meditation centers, sometimes a part of an ancient monastery, take in guests for a few days, but other specially constructed and maintained retreats for those who seek a radical retreat, physically and spiritually, are found in many parts of Sri Lanka. Of very simple and basic construction, with no embellishment to distract the senses, these usually occupy some of the most stunning geographical locations in the country. The minimal life of a monk is reflected in the spartan spaces.

The luxuriant vegetation and the beautifully manicured landscape of the island, especially where the main occupation of paddy cultivation is prevalent, makes it easy to imagine a life of plenty and therefore a possibility for retreating from it into one of contemplation of that landscape. The sheer abundance of nature can easily make one believe that one is in a magical land of lotus-eaters, a far cry from the hubbub of modern life. It is this combination of meditation and landscape that draws the many visitors to Sri Lanka.

One of the earliest resorts of modern times is the hill station Nuwara Eliya. Here, in a beautiful valley hidden in the highest hills of the island, the British created a miniature version of Scotland to which they would retreat from the heat of the lowlands. Today, Nuwara Eliya has lost many of its charms, but it still attracts armies of Sri Lankan holidaymakers in the April season. Colonial style survives in the corridors of the Hill Club and on the verandas of the Golf Club.

Although historically most Sri Lankans have taken the landscape of the island for granted, there is a long tradition of garden design and the building of gardens for pleasure. One example is the astonishing water garden of Sigiriya built, according to legend, by King Kassaypa in the fifth century. Two modern examples of the "pleasure garden" are the gardens created by Bevis Bawa and his architect brother Geoffrey.

The arrival of the long-haul jet in the 1960s brought a new kind of tourism to Sri Lanka. Amongst the earliest purpose-built commercial resorts, the Bentota Beach Hotel, designed by Geoffrey Bawa and built on a promontory in Bentota, held the magic until

BELOW
A giant frangipani dominates the northern terrace of Lunuganga, the garden estate of the late Geoffrey Bawa (page 154). Planted at the very inception of the garden in 1947 as two small branches, the tree was trained by Bawa to provide a perching site for the peafowl he once kept on the estate. The two nineteenth-century garden statues define the edge of the terraces, which drop steeply to the water garden and lake below.

recently. Its vocabulary of vernacular materials used with great sympathy on a modern building type was widely emulated across Asia. The same spirit is seen in Bawa's other works, including the unforgettable Triton Hotel, with its illusion of the sea sweeping into the lobby.

The rise of mass tourism was halted during the late 1980s by the eruption of civil war. But as peace returned to Sri Lanka, a new sort of tourism emerged, and small boutique hotels appeared to cater to the tastes of discerning travellers. This, in turn, encouraged nomadic souls to seek a permanent home in Sri Lanka. This trend has led to a decade of private house building.

The contemporary use of vernacular building materials in a particular combination has resulted in a recognizably Sri Lankan resort style. As in much of the rest of Asia, the reuse of vernacular building traditions to articulate modern needs has resulted in these buildings becoming well rooted in the place. Roofs covered by half-round terracotta tiles, plastered walls washed in a combination of lime wash and yellow ochre or *samara*, combined with trees bearing white frangipani, complete the picture of the Sri Lankan resort

or retreat. Visitors to the island invariably take back with them this memory of tile, white lime wash and frangipani.

Here, too, the syncretism that is part of the Sri Lankan ethos is evident. For none of these elements are entirely indigenous to Sri Lanka. Half-round terracotta tiles were introduced from Iberia via the Arabs and the Portuguese; the lime wash is local; the frangipani is native to South and Central America. However, the combination in which they appear within the actual spaces is inimitably Sri Lankan. Add to this terracotta tile or stone floors, white sarong-clad staff padding gently around in the warm, humid air, thick with the scent of frangipani or night-blooming Queen of the Night, and you have the essential ingredients of Sri Lankan resort style. Suites of rooms, their doorways in line with each other, invariably start and end in an outside space. Outdoor eating and living spaces predominate, with the building itself being merely a pavilion for use in inclement weather. Inside, the best exude the simplicity of a monastic retreat, with little to come between the people and the landscape, which is often the object of contemplation.

BELOW
The dining space under a giant rock in the Boulder Garden (page 172) includes a series of steps that lead up to a second polished concrete platform where one can also relax. Both areas overlook the forest and reflecting pool that defines the edge of the inhabited world.

Lunuganga

BENTOTA | ARCHITECT: GEOFFREY BAWA

Lunuganga is the legendary garden estate of architectural maestro Geoffrey Bawa. Started as a garden in 1947 on the island's west coast, Bawa spent forty years transforming an abandoned rubber estate into this tropical idyll, with elegant Italianate gardens, courtyards, pools, walkways, pavilions, and inspirational views over the surrounding lake and jungle. It is experiments here that first led to his taking up architecture as a profession, and throughout his life it was his laboratory and muse, "a place of many moods, the result of many imaginings, offering a retreat to be alone or fellow-feel with friends." Translated as "Salt River," the property lies on a promontory into a backwater of the Bentota River in spectacular setting as a "garden within the greater garden that is Sri Lanka." The garden is composed around an old plantation bungalow from the 1930s as a series of Arcadian vistas in a tropical setting.

Inspired by Bawa's many journeys and experiences of gardens in the East and West, Lunuganga remains a unique experience of a truly tropical Asian modern garden, a suite of serene outdoor rooms set amid the wilder wilderness of Sri Lanka. The main vista connects the view of the backwater through the main corridor of the house itself. To the south, it draws the eye past a kitchen Ming jar placed in the middle distance under a *moonamal* tree to a distant *dagaba* on the hill, while to the north, a pot under a frangipani frames the view of the lake and sky. Other vistas look over carefully tended rice paddies that become a foil to sculpted frangipani trees on small terraces, or stands of rubber trees framing a row of Ming jars on the edge of a pond in the field of jars. Small pavilions and eclectic sculptures punctuate the garden, particularly the leopard and cement ball that flank the water gate. Many walkways through the dense vegetation bring into focus unexpected views and make for contemplative walks.

RIGHT
The edge of the northern terrace overlooks the water garden and lake beyond. The island, purchased by Bawa in the 1970s to save it from destruction by an ill-conceived village expansion program, is now an official bird sanctuary.

The plantation house itself was completely transformed by turning it back to front. It is furnished with an eclectic mix of *objets d'art* chosen with the architect's meticulous eye. Seventeenth-century Indo-Portuguese chairs sit comfortably with twentieth-century paintings and sculptures, and a nineteenth-century garden sculpture frames a vista from a veranda lit by a locally made copper copy of a Paul Hennigson pine cone lamp.

Several other pavilions are scattered throughout the estate, including the romantic Glass Room, a long, thin, completely glazed-in guest room set above the entrance court. Waking up in it is akin to being in a tree. The Garden Room, assembled from old building parts, is a meticulous essay in the reuse of old material. The gallery, a former cowshed, and the henhouse, date from a period in the political history of Sri Lanka when the estate was very much a farm!

Lunuganga lives on today as testimony to a great architect, who not only enjoyed life in this bucolic setting, but made full use of it to make a decidedly important contribution to Asian and world architecture.

LEFT
The bathroom moves seamlessly from inside to out, where the shower comes off the fern-filled wall. A nineteenth-century sculpture stands guard at the door to the inside.

BELOW
Appointed with antique furniture, sculpture and art from Bawa's collection, the sitting room in the old plantation house is both elegant and intensely personal. The centrepiece is a nineteenth-century chandelier brought in as hand luggage by the architect's French cousin as a house-warming gift in 1949! The buffalo head chair by the Georgian ebony table was an eccentricity of a nineteenth-century British planter. The art is all twentieth century and includes the Trojan horse, a sculpture by Australian artist Donald Friend, and paintings by Sri Lankan artists Ivan Pieris and Raju and Indian artist Ranmanujam.

ABOVE
The southern terrace that overlooks the great lawn is the entrance to the main house at Lunuganga and a favorite breakfast place. Canvas directors' chairs are arrayed around an old cast-iron table. At the end of the terrace, peeping out of a niche overgrown with a strangling fig and other tropical foliage is a second-century Roman head.

LEFT
The veranda sitting area was once the entrance porch of the original estate house. Two built-in sofas and a couple of eighteenth-century corner chairs surround a cement table lined with terracotta tiles. The planting brings the outside in. An old fan overhead helps circulate air.

LEFT
The Sandella or Garden Room was constructed in 1983, the beginning of the twenty-year civil war in Sri Lanka. Formed almost entirely of materials salvaged from demolished buildings, it is a meticulous study in light, structure and proportion—all fundamentals of good architecture. Decorative objects include a seventeeth-century statue of Madonna and wooden toy racing cars made by a local toy manufacturer, arranged on a single plank of *para mara* (*Samanea saman*), which acts as a work table, the only such one on the estate. Two eighteenth-century Burgermaster chairs (one still able to swivel) provide seating. The bell and the Bishop's chair in the corner came from the local church, demolished because of a shortage of worshippers.

A mural in the Bridge House by Geoffrey Bawa's friend, artist Laki Sena-nayake. The fiery scene, from Greek mythology, belies the peace and seren-ity of Cinnamon Hill, a two-bedroom studio, to which it opens out.

RIGHT
Early morning sun streams into the Roman Pavilion on the western terraces of the estate. The slatted chair was originally designed by Geoffrey Bawa for his Kandalama Hotel.

RIGHT
Dappled sunlight lights
up the entrance court that
is overlooked by a satyr
molded on a pot, which
was designed by the artist
Donald Friend and Bawa's
brother Bevis.

BELOW
The entrance to the San-
della or Garden Room
is flanked by antique columns rescued from an old
building, and is almost
completely covered by a
Ceylon ironwood tree. The
vista through the building
into the lush vegetation
beyond is a hallmark of the
architect's work, where
what is seen from a building is often more important
than the building itself.

LEFT
Early light throws into
sharp silhouette an ancient
stone lingam and *dan* trees
against the paddy fields,
part of the water garden
on the western end of the
broad walk.

ABOVE
A Dutch-period door marks
the entrance to the Glass
Room above the entrance
court. Copper carriage
lamps of a nineteenth-
century design, light up
the steps at night.

Kandalama Hotel

DAMBULLA | ARCHITECT: GEOFFREY BAWA

Occupying a unique site in the cultural heartland of Sri Lanka, the Kandalama Hotel was built amidst great environmental controversy. It has now come to epitomize a new trend in hotel architecture and management that is fast taking over the globe. Awarded many environmental awards, the hotel derives its special status from being a building where the architecture—especially from the inside—almost entirely disappears. The landscape dominates it from every angle, including the bathrooms, and is literally taking over the building. Designed by the legendary architect Geoffrey Bawa for the hotel arm of the conglomerate Aitken Spence, he once contemplated what it would be like, if many, even greater works from the past, succumbed to the onslaught of the jungle that surrounded them and became the habitation of bears and leopards rather than visiting tourists. One sometimes feels this is already happening at Kandalama.

The magnificent entrance and reception set the tone for the interiors, which in many ways are not interiors at all. A huge expanse of flat concrete bridges a rock and a building hugging another rock to provide shelter for the reception desk, an old singed beam of Ceylon ironwood (*Messua ferrea*). Where the outside ends and the inside begins is never

clear as a sweep of living rock forms one of the walls and continues through the entrance passage to arrive at the reception lounge and pool deck from where there is a spectacular view of the fifth-century rock fortress of Sigiriya, 9 miles (15 km) away.

The austere approach to the interiors, while appearing rather spartan to some, only helps to emphasize the majesty of the landscape beyond. The conscious effort to keep references to the past out of the building acts as a neutral foil on which to project images of the past that a typical tourist arriving at the hotel from the cultural triangle would have observed. The simple palette of concrete frame structures and black aluminum glazing creates simple volumes and spaces to inhabit, which hardly make any demands on the occupants. The hotel, as Bawa once observed, is "merely a belvedere" from which to observe the sweeping panorama of landscape and history laid before it. The fourth-century reservoir, the distant fortress rock of Sigiriya, the rocky eminence of Dambulla with its first-century caves and eighteenth-century paintings and the high pinnacles of Ritigala with a second-century forest monastery at its base, remind one of a thousand and more years of drama and intrigue enacted in the landscape.

ABOVE
The terrace at the end of the approach ramp to the hotel, a sweeping plane of roof placed across a natural gap in the landscape, forms a forecourt to the reception area. Forty feet (12 meters) above the lake, the panorama beyond is gradually revealed on the ascent up the ramp on the right. Wherever possible, the existing rocks on the site were left undisturbed during construction of the hotel.

RIGHT
Two of the hotel's three sections are built on tall stilts that avoid disturbing the flow of rainwater. Jungle creepers pulsing with life climb up the five-story front of the bedroom wings, virtually engulfing the building. The wild vegetation on the roof garden helps reduce thermal gain into the building and provides a terrace for unique rooftop jungle activities.

RIGHT
A huge roof beam from a nineteenth-century building in Colombo struck by fire in 1984, forms a magnificent reception counter. Steel sleeves cover the singed edges. A print motif painted on the wall behind, inspired by an old hand-block printed *somana* cloth, glows in the evening sun.

BELOW
The entrance to the hotel is a huge sheltering roof reminiscent of a cave from the inside but indistinguishable from its surroundings on the outside. The texture of the living rock forming one wall of the entrance corridor is an interesting contrast to the smooth polished plaster of the other wall and the polished Indian *kadappa* stone on the floor.

LEFT
The main dining room overlooks Kandalama Lake on one side and a great overhanging rock on the other. Copies of eighteenth-century Dutch colonial Wolfendhal chairs are arranged under giant metal representations of traditional votive trees often found in miniature and made as offerings in Buddhist shrines.

BELOW
From the main lounge, visitors enoy panoramic views of Kandalama Lake. The lounge itself is simply furnished with clean-lined modern sofas and table lamps, paired with reproduction nineteenth-century cane chairs, all chosen to enhance the timeless nature of the space.

ABOVE AND LEFT
The dramatic lines of the swimming pool are in sharp contrast to the lake and hills beyond. The clearly articulated geometry of the modernist hotel, steadily being smothered by vegetation, rises above the tangle of tropical monsoon forest. The dining room and staircase are visible in the middle distance. The bedroom wings are on the far end.

RIGHT
The cave-like entrance to the hotel bridges a gap in the landscape and is reminiscent of the cave temples abounding in the surrounding area including the magnificent Dambulla caves.

OVERLEAF
Reflected sky on polished stone gives an illusion of the lake sweeping into the lounge, which seamlessly melds with the outside.

The Boulder Garden

KALAWANA | ARCHITECT: LALYN COLLURE

The Boulder Garden hotel, set amidst the lofty mountains of the UNESCO world heritage rainforest reserve of Sinharaja and the fertile rice and tea terraces of the southwest lowlands, follows the ancient Sri Lankan tradition of occupying natural sites by slight human intervention. The magnificent boulder-strewn site is used sensitively to provide accommodation for a mere handful of guests. The main man-made features include the addition of stone staircases to allow for easy access to the different levels and the creation of flat areas between rocks to accommodate a restaurant and other usable spaces.

The hotel is approached via a rough road through a plantation, which ends in a clearing on the edge of the tropical rainforest. The entrance is marked by a huge rock sheltering a cascade of water and an adjacent staircase leading into the dense forest. The path meanders through a series of platforms and levels between trees and huge boulders until it reaches the reception and entrance lounge under a

group of rocks. From here, winding stone steps and deep stone-block corridors lead to other parts of the hotel, including the ten bedroom suites, arranged in four rising tiers on the site. Local granite walls, huge timber beams, polished cement floors and metal-grilled windows contribute to the monastic feel of the suites.

The stone dining room, with adjoining lounge, is perhaps the most stunning place at the Boulder Garden. It is simply a flat platform made of plain mirror-polished concrete beneath the largest overhanging rock, with an almost flat bottom, on the site. The platform is surrounded by a reflecting pool that defines its edge and separation between the wild jungle and the inhabited space. A slightly elevated platform under the same rock forms the lounge. A swimming pool, fed by rain and spring water, stretches out from here into the wilderness, surrounded by a stone-paved terrace and the huge trees of the rainforest. The feeling of bathing in a forest pool is one of unique communication with the environment.

ABOVE
Water cascades down part of the staircase entrance to the Boulder Garden at the side of a huge granite boulder. This boulder sets the tone for the entire hotel, which follows in every respect the ancient tradition of rock and boulder gardens of Sri Lanka.

RIGHT
Lamp niches on the face of the pool bar light up the pool terrace at night.

RIGHT
The bright blue window shutters of the guest accommodation pick up the bluish tinge of the local granite.

FAR RIGHT
A dramatic corridor leads from the main public areas to the guest accommodation. Lamps in niches on the retaining wall light up the way.

RIGHT
The rain- and spring water-fed swimming pool, dappled by day and lit by night, stretches out into the forest from the warm glow of the dining room under the rock overhang. The shady, quiet surroundings are a sanctuary of serenity and beauty in this secluded hideaway, punctuated only by the occasional malarkey of monkeys and the honk of hornbills.

Kahandakanda

GALLE | ARCHITECT: BRUCE FELL-SMITH

The main organizing element in the architecture of Kahandakanda is a Luis Baraggan-like 260 foot (80 meter) saffron-colored wall that runs along the length of the site and acts as a divider between views across the tea and jungle and Koggala Lake in the distance. Glassless openings in the wall frame views on both sides. Most of the movement within the complex is along or across the wall. The large trees on the site also help to confer a sense of place.

The contemporary retreat, set on a prominent bluff 5 miles (9 km) from Galle, comprises a series of simple free-standing pavilions set around a swimming pool along or on either side of the saffron wall. The wall provides the necessary privacy between the individual sleeping pavilions, whilst allowing coherence between them. The main living area consists of a large living pavilion and a dining pavilion at one end and a swimming pool and terrace with a vine-covered patio at the other. In addition, two large reflecting pools flank the walkway to the living area.

The living room is partially enclosed with walls and grid-patterned window openings that allow air to enter and circulate. The dining room, on the other hand, is totally open to the surrounding garden and views beyond the edge of the terrace. Each of the sleeping pavilions is also open to the outside, with spectacular views into the distance. All are constructed of the simple palette of materials inspired by the local architecture: plaster walls, polished cement floors, timber plank ceilings and timber framework with half-round terracotta tiles. The simple orthogonal geometry of the pavilions, along with the large expanses of water, create the type of serenity associated with a local monastic complex.

Mirroring the style of the interior designer owner, the décor throughout the resort stands out for its ethnic luxury and panache. The brilliant orange of the outside wall provides the most striking color contrast to the predominantly black-and-white theme. Most of the furniture comes from the Workshop in Bentota. Chairs are generally made of a stainless steel frame mounted with timber slats, usually teak, but equally often of the timber of the *kitul* tree or fishtail palm. Modern cane divans and chairs are complemented by a few well-chosen antiques and other artifacts.

PREVIOUS PAGE
Perched along the ridge adjacent to the sitting pavilion, the dining pavilion glows at dusk.

ABOVE
Black-and-white ticking complemented by cotton checked cushions cover a contemporary cane sofa at the back of the half-open sitting pavilion. The timber feet on the glazed coffee table come from a nineteenth-century passion play figure. The Buddha is modern gilded Thai. The lamps, from a collection by Swiss designer Rico Tarawella, are aluminum and stainless steel.

LEFT
A table for ten with a solid teak top and stainless steel bases lies in the center of the open-sided dining pavilion. The stainless steel and leather chairs, also designed by Rico Tarawella, are locally made.

LEFT
A modern batik hanging
by Ena de Silva hangs over
a contemporary console
flanked by reproduction
nineteenth-century chairs.
The cane box on the con-
sole is a traditional Sri
Lankan piece while the
boxes stacked below the
console are Burmese.

BELOW
Under its soaring timber
ceiling, the master bed-
room opens out to wide
vistas over the coconut
trees. Contemporary furniture inspired by colonial
models creates a sparse,
almost minimalist interior,
softened by the traditional
cotton mosquito net and
massed cushions. The
clean cement terrazzo floor
glows with a soft shine,
reflecting the sky on to the
ceiling above.

LEFT
The long swimming pool runs almost the entire length of the Kahanda-kanda villa resort outside of Galle (page 176), reflecting the walls and sky.

BELOW
The pavilions are set on the crest of the hill to take advantage of the views across the tops of the coconut palms. Indian slate pavers define the path to the formal sitting room and the entrance, which is flanked by an old hardwood tree and a fragrant frangipani.

BOTTOM
The Baragganesque wall cuts across the landscape providing the intial *parti pris* for the design, as well as the main organizing principle for the scheme.

The plain polished cement floors and soaring timber and tile roof of the main sitting room pavilion allude to Buddhist preaching halls of the eighteenth and nineteenth centuries. Local handloom fabrics from the design house Paradise Road soften contemporary cane and steel furniture. The day bed in the foreground, with its distinctive Paradise Road cushions, is antique ebony. The black aluminum grilles on the windows add to the black-and-white theme in the soft furnishings.

Brief

BENTOTA | ARCHITECT: BEVIS BAWA

Brief is the legendary garden estate of the late Bevis Bawa, artist and aide-de-camp to four governors of Ceylon and elder brother of famed architect Geoffrey Bawa. Located along the south coast near Bentota, close to Geoffrey's garden Lunuganga (page 154), the estate reputedly got its name from being part of a brief given to their father Benjamin Bawa, a prominent Sinhalese lawyer, for a case he had presented at the Supreme court of the then Ceylon. The estate, planted in rubber at the time, was eventually inherited by Bevis, the elder of his two sons, who went on to make a part of it a tropical paradise for his own pleasure. Now open to the public, the first Sri Lankan private garden to be so, it has become a place for people of all walks of life to wander around and wonder about the colorful life of the man who created it.

Unlike Geoffrey's attempts at Lunuganga to convert tropical wilderness into an Italian garden, Bevis's Brief is almost entirely Sri Lankan in concept and spirit and reflects his keen interest in horticulture. The garden has been designed as a series of compositions with a tight sequence of space surrounding the main house. A treasury of exotic plants fills the relatively small space, all arranged to ultimately give a feeling of tropical plentitude.

Access to the property is across a marsh and village. The road arrives at a forecourt planted in the middle with an exotic palm. The eccentrically designed gates with satyrs and plants growing on and off them are by the Australian artist Donald Friend, who lived and worked at the estate for several years. This leads through an avenue of sealing wax palms to another more enclosed court lined with bamboo, and the main entrance to the bungalow. The entry leads into a curved passage that climbs up several feet to the main

RIGHT
Light metal shelves holding a collection of Hindu temple bronzes from various periods form a light screen between the entrance hall and the living room. The antique turned columns frame the brilliantly lit garden beyond. This contrast of light and shade is part of the magic of tropical living.

entrance loggia. Here, at the top of the stairs is a painting by Friend, full of meticulous and mischievous observations of Ceylon life. The crumbling painting and loggia overlook meticulously crafted views of the upper garden through the virtually open house. Vine-covered pergolas hide the original lines of the house and fuse the internal spaces with the outside, making the outside as much a part of the complex of living spaces as the inside. The upper garden, as much of the rest of it, is a series of intimate enclosed gardens, each opening off a particular room and then connected to each other, through doorways and gates, including the brick built moon gate connecting the garden of the master bedroom with the terrace of the main living space. Another such garden contains the bathing space for the guest in that room, a grotto with glassy-eyed satyr spewing water to shower from. Other amusing sculptures abound in the upper garden.

Inside, the original structure of the colonial plantation bungalow has been transformed beyond recognition. Antique furniture, art, sculpture and photographic memorabilia are all testimony to Bevis Bawa's good taste and his enjoyment of life.

ABOVE
The back veranda of the guest suite is a tranquil refuge among a riot of lush green vegetation. Antique turned columns support a simple corrugated cement sheet roof above a floor laid with terracotta tiles. An old Dutch planter's armchair is paired with a modern reproduction of the classic steel frame and leather butterfly chair.

LEFT
A sculpture of a young man is silhouetted against light streaming in from the main entrance door on the stairs leading to the hall.

FAR LEFT
Vine-clad pergolas extend the main loggia into the garden. Antique furniture blends harmoniously with Bevis's collection of art, including exquisite sketches by Laki Senanayake.

LEFT
The front door to the main house is set in a large bamboo hedge encircling the paved driveway, its roof hidden under a magnificent sprawling white bougainvillea.

BELOW
The depths of the inner sitting room, shaded by vine-clad pergolas, provide a cool retreat from the harsh midday sun. A nineteenth-century rattan sofa sits comfortably alongside cotton upholstered chesterfields, a modern travertine-topped coffee table and side tables formed of traditional Sri Lankan brass betel trays. Books and sculptures line the walls.

LEFT, RIGHT AND BELOW
Details of a mural by Australian artist Donald Friend in the entrance hall of the bungalow, illustrating Sri Lanka as the favored site of the Hindu god Skanda. Bevis Bawa had met the artist on a ship sailing from Colombo to Italy in 1949 and had invited him to stay when next in Colombo. Friend took up the offer in 1957 and stayed for several years. He built a studio in Bevis's garden and experimented prolifically with various media—bas relief tiles, painted doors, gold-leaf paintings, aluminum sculptures and murals—many of which remain at Brief as mementoes of his friendship with Bevis.

The Club Villa

BENTOTA | ARCHITECT: GEOFFREY BAWA

Set in the middle of a coconut plantation, a stone's throw away from the beach at Bentota, the Club Villa was originally built in 1979 by the architect Geoffrey Bawa as a beach house for the present owners, who were then managers of another hotel further up the beach. Since then, the original four bedrooms, living room, dining room and staff areas have been expanded to a sixteen-bedroom beach inn. Although not a building of the colonial era, the inspiration for its current form—the traditional combination of plaster walls, stone and cement floors and half-round tiled roofs, and the use of salvaged building materials and period furniture—is decidedly colonial.

From the driveway, a veranda enveloped in stunning pink bougainvillea leads to a small entrance court lined with black-and-white photos by Sri Lankan photographer Lionel Wendt. A garden door leads off this to the main lounge, which is set in a beautiful courtyard containing a small reflecting pool fed by water from a huge steel bowl. The far end of the lounge opens out to the garden, a small swimming pool and the sea beyond. The sweeping manicured lawns, the soporifically

ABOVE
Classic colonial-style cement posts and salvaged timber balusters frame the view from the sitting room of immaculate lawns and coconut palms.

LEFT
A window niche in a bedroom overlooks the brightly lit garden beyond. The chairs are an adaptation of the 1960s design used extensively in hotels designed by Geoffrey Bawa at that time.

RIGHT
Majestic antique turned columns hold up a tiled roof on the sea side of the detached bedroom block. The balcony in front is a quiet and tranquil spot for reading or relaxing by day or listening to the tropical night sounds.

RIGHT
In the original sitting room designed by Geoffrey Bawa, an antique lamp lights up part of a wall mural in biro and permanent marker by Sri Lankan artist Laki Senanayake.

BELOW
A hallmark yellow ochre wall provides a backdrop to an eighteenth-century chest, a modern granite Ganesh from Sri Lanka and a lamp made from an old furniture leg.

ABOVE
The main sitting room, with its blue-tinted cement tiles, contains an eclectic mixture of objects. Bright cotton cushions accessorizing the built-in seat are color co-ordinated with the modern reproduction from an Indian Jain/Cosmic painting. The white-painted coffee table, a combination of a modern top and eighteenth-century legs, is flanked by chairs of nineteenth-century design. The white trimmed timber doors are typical of the colonial period.

RIGHT
A vista of old wood-turned columns leading to the open dining area culminates in an Indian bronze image of Ganesh, the elephant god, dancing.

swaying coconut trees and two large barringtonia trees are a study in mimimalism.

A passage alongside a row of ground-floor bedrooms and a courtyard planted with Rafis palms leads to the colonnaded dining room, furnished with elegant British-period furniture. In an eccentric twist, one of the walls is painted a bright yellow! Other bedrooms are arranged above the lounge, bar and dining room, and in an entirely detached block built closer to the sea. The interiors of the bedrooms are meticulously decorated with local handloom materials and art by local artists. The furniture, as in all the other areas, is either original or copies of classic pieces of colonial and modern design. Because each type of bedroom is furnished in a slightly different way and also has a different aspect, the inn feels very much like a rambling old colonial mansion built over several centuries although it has been only a mere ten years between the building of the original house by Geoffrey Bawa and the later additions.

A Garden in the East

TRINCOMALEE | ARCHITECT: UNKNOWN

ABOVE
A small Balinese statue pays homage in the guest courtyard, which is filled with water plants.

Between November and January each year, the Maha Vehi or "great rains" bring a deluge to green the land along the northeast coast of Sri Lanka. For the rest of the year, the dry climate makes for the typical monsoon forest and vegetation characteristic of the area, except in one place. North of Trincomalee is a garden in which the emerald green of the island lingers throughout the year in a lush evocation of the tropical idyll. Lovingly created over a period of twenty years, the garden represents a myriad of ideas from various garden traditions, fused to become the retreat for an artist and her partner. A series of walkways and vistas, arbors and pergolas drip with tropical vegetation, creating a garden for the mind and a feast for the eyes. The house itself opens into the garden and becomes one with it, and is indeed the centerpiece of life in this Utopian enclave.

The garden is accessed along a broad gravel road shaded by rows of trees and shrubs. Seemingly simple pavilions make up the residential part of the estate, but the way the internal spaces open out to the surrounding gardens is remarkable. Simple concrete screens, painted white in many places, allow the buildings to breathe. They also allow the garden to be all-pervasive. The house becomes a covered garden within the greater open garden.

The main living space is a pavilion open to two sides of the garden off which the other living areas and service areas open. Elegant cloth-covered furniture is complemented by beautiful art works, some by the artist herself, others by her close artist friends. Wherever possible, the bedrooms, too, are directly and fully open to the garden as are the bathrooms.

The garden itself is organized about two axes, one running through the center of the house towards the sea, the other a cross axis to this one. They alone make sense of the profusion of growth in this most unlikely place.

POSTSCRIPT: On December 26th, 2004, "a wall of grey water with a little crest of white on top" washed it all away, as it did the lives of many others who lived on the coast around Sri Lanka.

LEFT
Encased in a simple cement shell, the bedroom is a cool oasis amidst a plethora of plants that greet the occupants at every turn. At one end of the room, Balinese masks watch over the bathtub, lined in mosaic tiles, which is set into the floor.

RIGHT
A splendid stand of bamboo (*Bambusa vugaris*) surrounded by alocasia plants marks the edge of the formal living terrace.

BELOW
Concrete screens moderate the sun streaming into the main living space, which is open on two sides to the garden, while allowing breezes to flow through. The bamboo-slatted ceiling, cement-tiled floor, cotton-covered furniture, warm-toned painting of the garden and ethnic artifacts all add to the charm of this simple room.

LEFT
Early sun streams into the studio through the stands of bamboo on the edge of the main living terrace, lighting up the artist's work table and an antique brass water carrier from northern Sri Lanka. The table itself is a single plank of *para para* wood.

ABOVE
A plain muslin mosquito net hangs above the bed at the other end of the bedroom, complemented by a colorful painted cloth temple hanging from India. The window above the wooden sideboard looks over the main living room terrace and pergola.

RIGHT
The house, which merges seamlessly and sensitively with the environment, is a study in simplicity. Bougainvillea covers most of the roof of the house, here seen from the back end. Other plants such as Roheo and Agave grow in great abundance on the lawn.

Aluvihare Walauwe

ALUVIHARE, MATALE | DESIGNER: ENA DE SILVA

Ancient seats of aristocratic families are often perceived as staid and old-fashioned places full of family heirlooms carefully preserved as a memorial to past glory. The Walauwe or Manor House at Aluvihare, Matale, in the northern foothills of the central massif, is a far cry from this. Although it is full of priceless heirlooms, it is lived in with a freshness and gusto that is hard to match. Its owner, Ena de Silva Aluvihare, is also an artist. She works mainly within the medium of batik and traditional Kandyan embroidery—both crafts which she has helped to resurrect in Sri Lanka by establishing co-operatives with village women. Her house is a crucible for experimentation in several of her thoughts and is akin to one of her magnificent works.

The old house, built by Ena's father to replace an older family seat, is of modern origin. Its setting overlooking the Matale valley and looking across at the Knuckles Range to the east is nothing short of breathtaking. Having moved to the old house from her Colombo residence, No. 5, Alfred Place, built by architect Geoffrey Bawa (page 122), Ena has transformed its interior into a veritable kaleidoscope of color, form and shape. Although at first glance it appears to be an untrameled display, it is clearly a disciplined approach to making an interior. Every surface is embroidered and decorated and no wall or ceiling has escaped attention. Ancient block-printed cloths hang alongside modern painted walls and handicrafts, while priceless antique furniture vies for attention with magnificent embroidery and needlework. The interior is, in fact, not very different from the completely painted walls and ceilings of eighteenth- and nineteenth-century Kandyan temples where no surface is spared the attention of the artist.

ABOVE
Soft morning light catches the lush vegetation around the lily pond in the garden. Three morning blooming water lilies greet the sun.

RIGHT
Superb Sri Lankan food is
served to visiting guests
at the Alu Kitchens One,
an enterprise of the craft
workshop on the premises.
Here, the table is set in
a veranda overlooking the
rich home garden filled
with jack, areca nut, coconut and other fruit trees.

BELOW
An exuberant collection
of exotic codieatum species
and other plants form a
border along the front of
the house. The shadow
of a giant tamarind softens
the early morning sun on
the house.

The entrance to the main living space is through the door to the right of the arrangement of wax flowers—made in the craft shop on the premises—sitting atop an eighteenth-century chest. A collection of Indo-Portuguese furniture is lost beneath embroidered cushions and throws, as are the dining table and chairs. Paintings on the walls and columns, based on designs from fragments of original painting on wood in the ceilings of seventeenth-century temples, meld into the painted surface. Other walls are covered by old trade cloths, some block-printed in Sri Lanka and others from India used in the East India trade. Batik reproductions of the county flags of the Kandyan kingdom hang down over the dining area.

The house, which sits on the edge of a high escarpment, is arranged about two axes. The main entrance axis runs through the central living spaces to the temporary Cadjan shed veranda at the back, while the cross axis links the two side wings of the house with the bedrooms and kitchens. From the platform of the front garden, filled with plants of almost every shape and color, the house is entered through large glass doors. A handsome Dutch-period chest topped by an elaborate arrangement of plastic and wax paper flowers forms a "screen" between the entrance and the central dining table. On either side are two intimate sitting areas filled to overflowing with heirloom antique chaise longues and chairs. The furniture is piled high with cushions and every imaginable type of cloth work, from embroidery to batik and crochet!

The dining table is placed at the meeting of the two axes, where there once was a wall and a dark corridor. The wall was removed and what is left of it is supported by two antique columns. The corridor is present as an alcove in the ceiling, which is hung with batik flags representing the various regions of the Kandyan provinces. The table setting changes from time to time in color and texture. However, it never fails to bear a highly elaborate arrangement of dry, wax and fresh flowers placed on at least five layers of tablecloth. The table is set at all times, with fresh hibiscus in finger bowls announcing every meal, a fitting setting for the magical meals of traditional rice and eighteen curries that are constantly served at the table.

A cloth-lined lounge with a large English oak table is located behind the dining area. The cloths themselves are old trade cloths from the East India trade, pinned on to the walls and ceiling. Further elaborately covered furniture is presided over by a magnificent Dutch-period cupboard encrusted with typical Kandyan brass work. The Cadjan roofed veranda outside this space extends the living area into the lush back garden, where there is a profusion of plants to equal those in the front garden, and links the main house to the garage and outhouses.

Each of the three bedrooms is decorated in Ena's inimitable style. As in the rest of the house, every imaginable surface is worked on. Each room also contains at least two large beds covered with magnificent embroidered bedspreads in traditional Kandyan designs. Antique Dutch *almirah* are complemented by brilliantly worked cupboards decorated with paper and paint.

RIGHT
Plastic flowers, fancy glass objects and an old brass candlestand on a patch-work table cloth, together with the painted cupboard in the background, set the tone for the decoration in the guest bedroom.

FAR RIGHT
Finger bowls with a floating hibiscus are *de rigeur* at the table. Here, batik table mats placed on a crocheted table cloth over another table cloth of batik form an eclectic setting.

OPPOSITE
Simple timber shelves in the brightly painted kitchen are crammed with the ingredients and utensils required to whip up a delicious Sri Lankan meal.

Apa Villas

THALPE | DESIGNER: CHAN SAU YAN

The coast at Thalpe, 3 miles (5 km) south of the port city of Galle, has become the setting for a string of beach villas for those out to avoid the urban pleasures on offer in the seventeenth-century fort. Thalpe, with its picture book coastline, has changed from a sleepy fishing village to a wall of villas looking out to the sea on the thin strip of land between the Galle Road and beach. Apa Villas, three colonial-style villas situated in a coconut grove, is one of these and is named by its owner in honor of the extremely successful series of travel guides he founded in the 1980s.

Like its counterpart Iluketiya in the hinterland, Apa Villas takes its inspiration from the simple vernacular building traditions of Sri Lanka. A minimal palette of coconut wood columns and plaster walls coupled with roofs of half-round terracotta tiles and plain polished cement rendered floors, allows the villas to blend harmoniously with their natural surroundings. Most of the furniture is built in, with handloom cushions in a subdued palette thrown in for comfort. Bathrooms, too, consist of minimal ceramic tiling with polished cement bowls set in cement vanity counters.

Entry to the elegant villas is through a courtyard open to the entrance court off the highway and into the main sitting area, which in turn opens into a veranda overlooking a lawn with coconut trees and the sea. A long infinity-edge lap pool appears to merge with the Indian Ocean beyond. The main sitting area contains two large built-in sofa seats and a stainless steel dining table, invariably adorned with an exotic flower arrangement. The two end walls are lined with bookshelves housing locally made artifacts as well as the entire collection of Apa guidebooks, whose spines form a tapestry of background color in the formal but stylish room.

All of the bedroom suites have built-in four-poster beds and an adjoining sitting area filled with a simple built-in ledge, day bed and sofa. The half-open bathrooms of the new guest villas are situated in verandas off the bedrooms, each overlooking its own courtyard.

Although there is a formal living and dining room, guests spend much of their time lounging on the wide verandas facing the sea, enjoying the monsoon winds, the swaying palms and the surf rolling into the shore.

ABOVE
The Apa Villas overlook a magnificent coral beach where stilt fishermen still sit. The complex, constructed from a simple palette of materials, originally comprised a simple two-bedroomed house on the beach to which two guest wings were later added, the first centerd on the long, slightly raised lap pool, and the other one a higher-roofed double-roomed pavilion at the far end of the garden.

RIGHT
The long lap pool, raised slightly above the level of the lawn, extends from the central veranda towards the sea and horizon, ending in a timber deck.

RIGHT
The formal sitting room-cum-reading room at Apa Villas is situated directly behind the entrance courtyard. It is also the venue for communal dinners on festive occasions. The built-in cement shelves are filled with small *objets d'art* and the entire set of Apa guides. The dining chairs originate from a Scandinavian design of the 1960s via the Geoffrey Bawa office and have been adapted with stainless steel and teak by the Swiss designer Rico Tarawella and made at the Workshop in Bentota. A small wooden canoe sits on top of the bookshelves.

BELOW
The deep, shady veranda with its broad overhanging roof, cool polished cement floors and timber columns is where the owners and their guests spend much of their time at Apa Villas.

ABOVE
The vernacular ambience is tempered in the bedrooms by the use of extensive built-in furniture. Here, the sitting area is almost entirely built in except for the modern teakwood coffee table. The neutral tones of the upholstery are offset by faux leopard skin and warm yellow cushions.

RIGHT AND FAR RIGHT
In the entrance courtyard, contemporary depictions of a Western gentleman holding a bird and a local grandee, both painted in the nineteenth-century southern style, form attractive backdrops to colonial chairs and polished floors.

Acknowledgments

For a book three years in the making, the list of persons to thank and acknowledge would obviously exceed the limitations of space allotted here. So we will restrain ourselves! First and foremost, our thanks to our editors and publisher who very kindly and patiently put up with us as we waited for the soft morning light to touch the weather-beaten surface on that particular day of the year in the second monsoon with wind blowing from the northeast.

Equally we wish to thank all the owners of the properties, whose unfailing patience and graciousness in letting us invade their privacy makes the book what it is. Since many of them specifically asked not to be mentioned, we remain silent on all their identities. Some we cannot go without mentioning, even if they want us not to. Anjalendran for his unfailing criticism and encouragement. We think we still fall far short of his high standards, but it motivated us to be clear about how we approached this book. Professor David Robson for his patient reading of the first drafts and being an indulgent host. Kaushik Mukkerjee, Priyanka Samaraweera, P. G. Dinesha Dilrukshi and Shiromi Rajapakse, whose hard work and company made our lives easier. And mostly to our families and friends for putting up with never-ending descriptions of a book that lately even they—firm believers in us— seemed to doubt would ever come out.